SELLING EUROPE TO THE WORLD

BLOOMSBURY VISUAL ARTS
Bloomsbury Publishing Plc
50 Bedford Square, London, WC1B 3DP, UK
1385 Broadway, New York, NY 10018, USA
29 Earlsfort Terrace, Dublin 2, Ireland

BLOOMSBURY, BLOOMSBURY VISUAL ARTS and the Diana logo are trademarks of
Bloomsbury Publishing Plc

First published in Great Britain 2023

Cover design by Catherine Wood
Cover image: Christian Dior Haute Couture Fall Winter 2018/2019, PFW, 2018.
(© Victor VIRGILE/Gamma-Rapho/Getty Images)

A catalogue record for this book is available from the British Library.

Library of Congress Cataloging-in-Publication Data
Names: Donzé, Pierre-Yves, author.
Title: Selling Europe to the world : the rise of the luxury fashion industry,
1980-2020 / Pierre-Yves Donzé.
Description: [New York] : [Bloomsbury Visual Arts], [2023] | Includes bibliographical
references and index.
Identifiers: LCCN 2022022340 (print) | LCCN 2022022341 (ebook) |
ISBN 9781350335776 (hardback) | ISBN 9781350335783 (paperback) |
ISBN 9781350335790 (pdf) | ISBN 9781350335806 (epub) | ISBN 9781350335813
Subjects: LCSH: Luxury goods industry--Europe. | Luxuries—Europe—Marketing.
Classification: LCC HD9999.L853 E8536 2023 (print) | LCC HD9999.L853 (ebook) |
DDC 338.4/7094—dc23/eng/20220523
LC record available at https://lccn.loc.gov/2022022340
LC ebook record available at https://lccn.loc.gov/2022022341

ISBN: HB: 978-1-3503-3577-6
       PB: 978-1-3503-3578-3
       ePDF: 978-1-3503-3579-0
       eBook: 978-1-3503-3580-6

Typeset by RefineCatch Limited, Bungay, Suffolk
Printed and bound in India

To find out more about our authors and books visit www.bloomsbury.com
and sign up for our newsletters.

SELLING EUROPE TO THE WORLD

THE RISE OF THE LUXURY FASHION INDUSTRY, 1980–2020

Pierre-Yves Donzé

BLOOMSBURY VISUAL ARTS

LONDON • NEW YORK • OXFORD • NEW DELHI • SYDNEY

CONTENTS

ILLUSTRATIONS

Figures

Illustrations

Charts

Tables

ACKNOWLEDGEMENTS

Luxury goods have always fascinated consumers, but in the 1980s and 1990s, a global luxury industry emerged that has made luxury goods ubiquitous, from fashion magazines and Hollywood productions to airport shops and city centers. Luxury goods have become the embodiment of globalized material culture. However, what is fascinating in the luxury industry is not so much the glamour of a Dior dress, a Louis Vuitton bag, or an Omega watch, but rather the ability of European companies—French companies in particular—to exercise almost unchallenged dominance in the global market. There are, of course, competitive European companies in many other industries, from automotive to biotechnology to finance to retail, but they are in direct competition with American and Asian companies and do not dominate these sectors. The originality of the luxury industry is its European character, although its outlets extend across the whole planet. What are the competitive advantages of European luxury companies? Why and how do they dominate the global market? These questions are at the heart of the research I have been conducting for several years. Initially, I was interested in understanding how Swiss watchmakers managed, during the 1980s and 1990s, to regain their position as world leaders against Japanese competitors. This interest led me to analyse the transformation of a manufacturing industry based on technological innovation into a luxury industry based on the exploitation of global brands.[1]

Subsequently, and thanks to collaborating with many colleagues and friends, I had the opportunity to enrich my reflections by taking an interest in new themes related to the luxury industry, notably distribution and department stores, the globalization of markets, the transformations of the fashion industry, as well as the role of urban and real estate development. I would like to express my sincere gratitude to Rika Fujioka (Kansai University, Osaka), Tomonori Inukai (Chuo University, Tokyo), Sotaro Katsumata (Osaka University), Koichi Nakagawa (APS online school), Kentaro Nobeoka (Osaka University), Véronique Pouillard (Oslo University), Joanne Roberts (Southampton University), Thierry Theurillat (Haute école de gestion, Neuchâtel), and Ben Wubs (Erasmus University, Rotterdam). The research with you has been a pleasure that I hope to continue in the years to come. I would also like to thank the participants of the graduate seminar in global business history that I have been leading for several years at Osaka University and which is devoted to the creative industries (design, luxury, and fashion). The exchanges and debates with students from diverse cultural backgrounds have contributed enormously to my reflections on the modern luxury industry.

This book owes a great deal to my friend Alain Cortat, director of Éditions Alphil (Neuchâtel, Switzerland) and my editor in the French-speaking world for more than ten years, for his very constructive suggestions and criticisms of the first draft of the manuscript. Thank you so much, Alain! This book was originally published in French in autumn 2021, by Éditions Alphil under the title *Vendre l'Europe au monde: L'industrie globale du luxe des années 1980 à nos jours*.

Finally, a special thank you to Hiroko and my daughters, Yuki and Natsu: you share my life and give me the love and energy I need every day to carry out my many projects.

I wrote this book during an exceptional year. Cancelled conferences and trips abroad, lockdowns, and working from home allowed me to concentrate on its preparation. The luxury industry itself was hit hard by the coronavirus disease 2019 (COVID-19), as were many other sectors, before experiencing a tremendous rebound phase. However, I have chosen not to discuss in detail the impact of this crisis here as it is still too soon to develop a sensible reflection based on clearly established data. Instead, the reader will find in these chapters the state of the global luxury industry on the eve of the COVID-19 crisis. I hope the book will contribute to a better understanding of the dynamics of this sector over the last four decades.

Osaka, April 2022

INTRODUCTION

In a book of interviews with Bernard Arnault published in 2004, Yves Messarovitch states that Arnault "is the one who invented a new industry in the world, the luxury industry." He then adds:

> It did not exist before, except through medium-sized craft companies. He is, in his field, a true creator, the revealer of an industry that has become, thanks to him, global.[1]

Admittedly, Messarovitch's book is highly hagiographic, its main objective being to showcase the managerial genius of one of the richest men in the world. However, he immediately points out an essential, perhaps the most important, characteristic of contemporary luxury: it is a new industry. The fact that it is based on the exploitation of old brands often leads one to imagine that it has crossed the centuries and that the continuity of brands and know-how constitutes its specificity. The contemporary discourse of companies, relayed by the work of historians and management researchers, insists on the historical continuity of luxury, which precisely confers on many brands their legitimacy to embody it.[2] However, the work of the historian is not only to try to reconstruct the permanence of phenomena such as artisanal know-how and the transmission of technical excellence. Historical knowledge also teaches the importance of ruptures, of the creative destructions dear to Werner Sombart and Joseph Schumpeter.[3] The creation of the LVMH Moët Hennessy–Louis Vuitton group in 1987 is certainly one of these turning points. It laid the foundations for a profound transformation of the luxury industry, now dominated by financial capitalism. The takeover of small family businesses in various luxury sectors, their integration into conglomerates and their transformation into global brands have profoundly transformed this industry since the 1980s and 1990s.

However, defining the precise boundaries of this sector of activity remains a major problem. Unlike other industries, which are defined by their products (automotive, beverages, electrical equipment, etc.), services (finance, consulting, etc.) or manufacturing processes (chemicals), luxury is defined by a market segment, the highest one. There are luxury products and services in almost every industry. Moreover, the difficulty is reinforced by there being no frontal opposition between luxury goods (intended for a small, wealthy elite) and mass-consumption goods. There are intermediate categories, such as accessible luxury or premium brands, which ensure continuity of market segmentation between exclusive luxury and mass products. Finally, luxury has a strong individual and subjective dimension, in the sense that its perception depends on factors that vary according to levels of economic development, cultures, and personal perception. Under these conditions, how can luxury be defined? There is still no consensus on this complex but essential question.[4] However, from the business history perspective adopted in this book, what matters is the willingness of firms to position themselves as manufacturers of luxury goods. Luxury management gurus Jean-Noël Kapferer and Vincent Bastien have made it clear that luxury brands require a marketing strategy based on fundamentally different principles from those influencing other types of goods. They list these principles as follows: product development without taking into account the desires of the customer; the absence of production cost considerations; the maintenance of production activities in the country of origin; the need to dominate the customer; the raising of prices to increase sales; advertising that does not serve to sell but to convey a message, etc.[5] The specificity of the marketing strategy exposed by Kapferer and Bastien has allowed value-added brands to increase. It is certainly a purist definition of a luxury strategy. While rarely followed to the letter by companies, it strongly inspires them and allows the identification of a corpus of actors involved in this industry and analyzed in this book.

Indeed, Arnault clearly articulates a philosophy of luxury management that is close. The objective of LVMH is summarized as the creation of "an economic reality from the ideas of the group's creators [...]."[6] With a fortune estimated at $12.2 billion when Messarovitch's book was published in 2004, Arnault was ranked twentifirst among the world's richest men by the American magazine *Forbes*. His main company, the LVMH group, was experiencing tremendous growth; its turnover had risen from €2 billion in 1987, the year it was founded, to 12.6 billion that year, allowing Arnault to enter the very select club of the world's richest men in the mid-1990s.[7] His meteoric rise has continued

Figure 0.1 Bernard Arnault at École Polytechnique, Paris, 2017.
Source: Wikimedia Commons, https://commons.wikimedia.org/wiki/File:Bernard_Arnault_(5)_-_2017.jpg

to the present day. Arnault is regularly mentioned in the world's press as one of the world's top three billionaires, with his exact rank changing with stock market fluctuations—he briefly became the world's richest man for the first time, ahead of Amazon boss Jeff Bezos, in May 2021.[8] Arnault was worth $82 billion in 2019, up from 3.1 billion in 1997. The luxury industry is not only new but characterized by extraordinary growth.

Estimates by the consulting firm Bain & Co. highlight the almost continuous expansion of the luxury consumer goods market (fashion, cosmetics, watches and jewelry, leather goods, and accessories) for over two decades (Chart 0.1). The global market size grew from €76 billion in 1996 to €281 billion in 2019. Growth has been on a general upward trend, with a slowdown in the early 2000s and a decline during the global financial crisis. The surge in demand for luxury goods has thus offered growth opportunities for many companies. It has also contributed to the transformation of this industry, as new organizational forms (conglomerates and listed companies) and new marketing strategies (distribution in mono-brand shops and construction of global brands) appear in this context.

However, while it is true that the luxury consumer goods market expanded rapidly after the 1990s, the extent of the increase lessened in the 2010s. A comparison with the growth of the global economy shows two main phases: a period of rapid expansion between 1994 and 2007, during which the luxury market grew from 0.31 percent to 0.38 percent of global GDP; and a period of relative stagnation after the global financial crisis

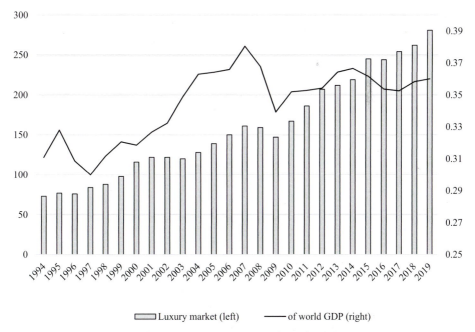

Chart 0.1 Evolution of the global luxury consumer goods market, billion euros, 1994–2019.
Source: Bain & Co. and World Bank.

(average of 0.36 percent of global GDP in 2010–19). Bain & Co.'s estimates, unfortunately, do not go back before 1994, but these figures show that the new industry created by Bernard Arnault and other entrepreneurs (such as Anton Rupert of Compagnie Financière Richemont, François Pinault of Kering, and Nicolas Hayek of Swatch Group) experienced almost two decades of consecutive growth after the foundations were laid. The contemporary luxury industry is an organizational innovation. Since 2010, it has become a more mature industry, based on a set of large, dominant companies, whose growth now depends on the global economy.

A key feature of the luxury industry is its domination by European brands and companies. Although the market is globalized, it is mostly controlled by French, Italian, British, and Swiss companies. The 2020 ranking of the world's biggest brands in terms of financial valuation, drawn up by the consulting firm Interbrand, includes eleven luxury brands: Louis Vuitton (17th), Chanel (21st), Hermès (28th), Gucci (32nd), L'Oréal (43rd), Cartier (73rd), Dior (83rd), Hennessy (91st), Tiffany (94th), Burberry (97th), and Prada (99th),[9] all of which are European except Tiffany. Luxury is even one of the few industries in which Europe has managed to maintain and strengthen its comparative advantage in the twenty-first century.[10] While other new industries, such as information and communication technology, are dominated by large American and Chinese companies, and old industries (automotive, chemical, machinery, metallurgy) are experiencing fierce competition between different regions of the world, luxury has the originality of being a profoundly European business. It is based on the exploitation and enhancement of cultural resources that make it possible to add emotional value to manufactured objects and sell them successfully around the world.

Since the 1990s, luxury has been the subject of a considerable number of academic studies and publications in the fields of management and history, which highlight particular aspects of this industry. There is no need to revisit this literature in this book. Many works are presented and used in the following chapters. Readers interested in a detailed analytical review of these publications should refer to my articles on this subject.[11] This book aims to provide a narrative that explains the conditions for the formation and development of the contemporary luxury industry from the 1980s to the present. It seeks to understand why and how European companies managed to establish themselves as major players in this sector.

The book is divided into two parts. The first deals with the triple industrial transformation that is at the origin of contemporary luxury (globalization of markets, creation of large multinational companies and construction of global brands). The second part presents an analysis of the main organizational models. Although largely dominant, the luxury conglomerate, embodied by LVMH, is not the only ideal type of company that exists in this sector. Other types of organizations, such as the independent family firm, industrial groups, companies with deep regional roots, and new companies, are discussed and their characteristics, competitive advantages, and weaknesses compared to the conglomerates presented.

As the archives of luxury companies are generally not available for the last four decades, the main sources for this book are annual reports of companies and associations, analyzes published by consulting firms, and official statistics on foreign trade. I have also used the *International Directory of Company Histories* series as a source for the factual history of the companies analyzed in the following pages. The currencies used to represent values are the euro and the US dollar. Where the source uses another currency, such as the Swiss franc, British pound, Japanese yen, or Indian rupee, the US dollar equivalent is calculated based on the average exchange rate and mentioned in the text.[12]

PART I
THE BIRTH OF THE GLOBAL LUXURY INDUSTRY

The contemporary luxury industry is the result of a triple transformation that took place during the 1980s and 1990s: the globalization of markets, the creation of large multinational companies, and the adoption of new marketing strategies. These three aspects are very closely linked (Chart 0.2).

First of all, the globalization of markets—that is to say, both the extension of luxury outlets to all the countries of the world and the integration of these various regions into a global market—increases the competition between brands and leads to a concentration within large multinational companies, whether they are conglomerates (such as LVMH) or independent firms (such as Giorgio Armani). Large companies allow brands to be present in the world's main markets. Furthermore, the growth in demand, induced by the globalization of markets, influences the marketing strategies of luxury companies, which respond by creating global brands based on a particular heritage. Finally, the large multinational company has many resources, both financial and human, and these make the new marketing strategies possible. In turn, the creation of global brands with a strong identity allows companies to diversify and create portfolios of complementary brands to rationalize their investments in logistics, real estate and financial services.

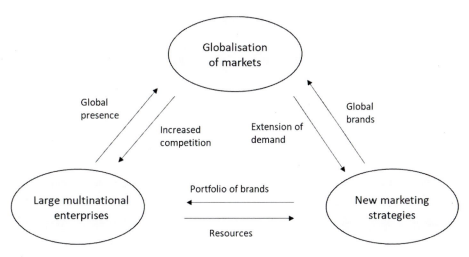

Chart 0.2 The triple transformation of the luxury industry.
Source: Author.

It should also be emphasized that this threefold industrial transformation has benefited primarily European companies, particularly French, Italian, and Swiss. The historical roots of Paris as a fashion capital, the traditions of craftsmanship and a certain—largely idealized—image of the European way of life form the basis on which global luxury brands have developed since the 1980s. The industrial transformation of luxury is analyzed in detail in the three chapters that make up this first part.

CHAPTER 1
GLOBALIZATION OF MARKETS

In 2008, at the *Financial Times Business of Luxury Summit* in Tokyo (an annual gathering of the major players in the luxury industry), the editor-in-chief of the British business daily declared in his opening speech that 94 percent of Japanese women in their twenties owned a Louis Vuitton item. The audience was amazed and seduced by this statement, even though a modicum of critical thinking would have exposed the figure as exaggerated and completely unrealistic.[1] Echoed by a host of commentators and self-proclaimed experts, its rapid spread throughout the fashion and luxury media worldwide is because it reinforced the myth that Japanese women love luxury brands. Nonetheless, Japan was the first non-Western country to become a significant market for the European luxury industry.

Admittedly, since the interwar period, the United States has been an important outlet for French haute couture and European luxury craftsmen.[2] From this point of view, they are the first non-European luxury market. However, there are two main reasons why America is not fundamentally a new market in terms of type of consumption. Firstly, it is worth recalling the cultural proximity between the white East Coast elites, who represent the heart of the American clientele, and the European haute bourgeoisie. Secondly, until the 1970s, European luxury companies targeted a niche market, whether American or European. The United States did not therefore play a particular role in the industrial transformation of European luxury. It is Japan that represents a real turning point, in the sense that, for the first time, the European luxury industry was confronted with a new cultural context and a new demand structure. This country has been instrumental in the globalization of luxury, with the 1980s being a turning point.

1.1 French leather goods exports

Foreign trade statistics provide a general perspective on the globalization of luxury markets since the 1960s. Let us take the example of French leather goods, which today represent, along with Hermès and Louis Vuitton, one of the best expressions of this sector. Chart 1.1 shows the growth of French leather goods exports from 1960 to 2018, in current euros, and the market shares of four major markets (United States, Japan, Hong Kong, and China). Three main phases can be distinguished.

Firstly, between 1960 and the early 1970s, it was a niche market. Exports were certainly on the rise but of low value (€17.1 million in 1960 and €36.6 million in 1970). Moreover, the anchoring in Western countries was extremely strong. The United States was the largest market (38.5 percent in the 1960s), and sales in Asia were almost non-existent. The European Community (EC) as a whole also represented a vital market (27.9 percent

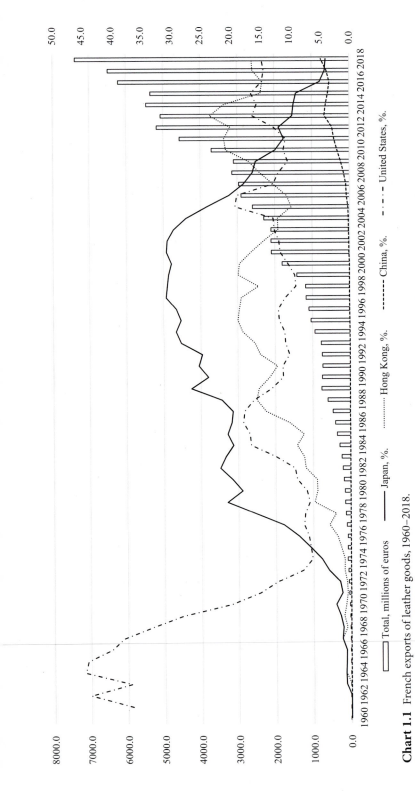

Chart 1.1 French exports of leather goods, 1960–2018.

Source: *Statistiques du commerce extérieur de la France* (1960–96) and COMTRADE (since 1997). All values have been converted into euros.

Legend: Total, millions of euros — Japan, %. ...... Hong Kong, %. ----- China, %. —·— United States, %.

in 1965). The EC was still the old world of luxury, dominated by small companies that offered exclusive products to the upper-middle classes of Western countries.

Secondly, 1975 to 2000 was a transitional period toward a strongly growing market increasingly dependent on East Asia. The value of exports reached €154 million in 1980 and 748 million in 1990, passing the billion-euro mark in 1995 and reaching 1.8 billion in 2000. The size of the global French leather goods market thus experienced a tremendous boom, and the 1980s appear to be a fundamental break. The increase was also due to the emergence of new markets. With US market share showing a dramatic decline, dipping to less than 10 percent in 1973–82, the increase was based on Japan. While its market share was less than 5 percent until 1974, within two years it had surpassed that of the United States, reaching 18.1 percent in 1980 and peaking at more than 30 percent in 1997–2003. Japan had a ripple effect on the emergence of other markets through tourism as its citizens brought back luxury goods from their travels, largely explaining the sharp rise in exports to Hong Kong in 1980–2000 and the US during the 1980s.[3]

The growing importance of the Japanese market was the result of strong economic growth and the rise of the yen in the 1970s and 1980s, embodied by the speculative bubble of 1985 to 1991, which made the Japanese the highest average-income people in the world. However, the consumption of luxury goods was not the only consequence of increased purchasing power. Social and cultural factors must also be taken into account, such as the appeal of high-quality handicrafts (which resonates with the new storytelling of the luxury industry), the westernization of lifestyles, the desire for social identification through branded consumption and, to return to the young Japanese women, the high incomes of singles who live with their parents until they marry. These "single parasites" were one of Louis Vuitton's main targets when the brand entered the Japanese market in 1978.[4]

Third, since 2000, Japan (having entered a phase of demographic ageing and economic stagnation) has seen its market share fall sharply (12.4 percent in 2010 and below 5 percent since 2016). Its decline follows that of Hong Kong in the first part of the 2000s. However, French leather goods exports have continued to soar, passing the €5 billion mark in 2012 and 7 billion in 2018. They now rely on a new clientele: the Chinese consumer. Its importance is less visible in the export statistics because the taxes on luxury goods in China lead Chinese nationals to make their purchases abroad. China's direct share, while low, is increasing, surpassing Japan's in 2018. The Hong Kong market was in a new growth phase until political instability in Hong Kong in 2013 kept Chinese tourists away. Their leather goods shopping then shifted to Singapore, London, and New York but was no longer directly observable through export data. This geographical splintering of shopping explains why the combined share of the four main markets, as shown in Chart 1.1, fell from over 55 percent in the 1990s to under 40 percent after 2016.

Beyond the numbers, the example of Louis Vuitton well illustrates how Japan became a major market and what role Japan played in the company's development. Until the 1970s, the commercial expansion of the trunk and travel goods company, founded in 1854, was limited by its family character. To maintain control of the company, the Vuitton family did not open up its capital and had few means to expand its sales network. It owned only two shops—one in Paris and one in Nice—and relied on independent importers and distributors to access foreign markets.[5] In 1977, Henri Racamier, a representative of the fourth generation, thoroughly reviewed the company and transformed the small family business into a multinational firm, concentrating on extending the network of shops and establishing a new communication policy based on sponsorship.[6]

Vuitton expanded in the Japanese market in this context.[7] The French leather goods manufacturer was already present through a contract with the importer Mitsui and the local distributor Sann Frères. However, in the second half of the 1970s, consumption in the Japanese market began to grow through a network of parallel importers who bought Louis Vuitton bags abroad and sold them at discounted prices in Japan. The French head office wanted to end such a practice, which was harmful to profits and brand image. To better control its presence in the country, Louis Vuitton opened an office in Tokyo in 1978, which was transformed a few years later into a subsidiary. It was responsible for imports, distribution, and marketing, working with the Seibu and Takashimaya department stores for sales. In 1978, Vuitton opened six shops in Japan, four of which were in department stores. This experience led it to open its first shop in the United States in 1980. In Japan, the number of boutiques increased from thirty-eight in 1999 to fifty-five in 2019.[8] These stores became essential places for transmitting to Japanese consumers the values that Vuitton intended to embody. They represented a major communication tool. For example, as early as 1978, Louis Vuitton Japan displayed a portrait of the founder and an old trunk to emphasize the historical roots (and therefore the legitimacy) of the company in the field of travel equipment and accessories. After 2000, Vuitton shops were designed by local architects as an expression of the firm's support for art and creativity. The flagship shop, opened in August 2002 in Tokyo's upscale Omotesando district, was designed by renowned architect Jun Aoki, who would later also renovate Vuitton shops in New York and Hong Kong. Bernard Arnault, the owner of LVMH, stated in his group's annual report that the Tokyo Omotesando shop was:

> one of the jewels in our network of shops, it is also a symbol of Louis Vuitton's exceptional success in the Archipelago and a testimony to its attachment to Japanese customers.[9]

The strategy implemented in Japan by Louis Vuitton in 1978 was very successful for more than two decades and contributed decisively to the growth of French leather goods exports in the country. Sales rose from 1.2 billion yen in 1979 ($5.5 million) to 35.3 billion in 1990 ($243.4 million) and 135 billion in 2002 ($1.1 billion). In 2002, sales represented 8.8 per cent of LVMH's total turnover and more than 25 percent of the fashion and leather division.[10] This strong increase was due to adapting to the Japanese market by developing new products specially designed for Japanese customers—the famous parasite singles. Louis Vuitton launched several handbag collections in Japan that were later used elsewhere in the world: Epi (1984), Saumur (1987) and Taiga (1994). The company collaborated with Japanese artists such as designer Takashi Murakami, who created a colorful version of the Monogram LV in 2002. Finally, to offer accessible

Figure 1.1 People waiting for their turn to get into a newly-opened Louis Vuitton store on Omotesando Avenue, Tokyo, Japan (2002).
Source: Getty Image, ID: 1366159
Credit: Junko Kimura / Stringer

products to low-income consumers attracted to the brand, Vuitton created many small accessories (keyrings, purses, etc.). This contributed significantly to the brand's reputation in the Japanese archipelago.[11]

1.2 Accessing the Japanese market

The example of Louis Vuitton raises the question of how to access a distant market. The consistency of the brand image requires control of distribution (price and image of goods), while the specificities and opportunities of the market lead to the development of particular products. For European luxury companies, the Japanese market was usually the first non-Western market to become important. The conditions of access evolved during the second half of the twentieth century and the first two decades of the twenty-first century. They highlight the major break in the 1990s.

Until the 1980s, foreign direct investment in sales was not fully liberalized. Moreover, the Japanese distribution system was complex, with several levels of local wholesalers and distributors, making it almost impossible for a foreign company to reach retailers on its own—cooperation with Japanese partners was necessary. In the 1960s, a few Western cosmetics companies, such as L'Oréal (1963) and Estée Lauder (1967), opened subsidiaries in Japan. A few watch and jewelry companies followed, such as Tiffany (1972), Boucheron

(1973), and Longines (1974), as well as fashion and leather goods manufacturers such as Louis Vuitton (1978), Chanel (1980), and Hermès (1983).[12] These companies specialized in importing luxury goods and selling them to local distributors. They also oversaw marketing activities in the country. However, these cases were exceptions. Most of the other luxury brands, which were small family businesses, did not have the means to open a subsidiary in Japan. They could choose one of two strategies: a licensing agreement for the manufacture of their products in Japan by a local partner or an import agreement with a trading company.

French haute couture houses use licensed production widely.[13] Christian Dior was a forerunner. In 1953, he signed a contract with the department store Daimaru to manufacture dresses under license. Many other department stores adopted this practice in the following years: Takashimaya with Pierre Cardin (1959), Matsuzakaya with Nina Ricci (1961), Mitsukoshi with Guy Laroche (1963), and Isetan with Pierre Cardin (1963). These business relationships began with the production of women's clothing and gradually extended to a wide variety of accessories.[14] Moreover, department stores were not only partners for licensed production in Japan but also for retailers who took over the sale of these products. Since the interwar period, they have been the promoters of Western material culture in Japan and are where Japanese consumers acquire these goods.[15] However, it is not only department stores that signed contracts with European fashion houses. Various textile and clothing manufacturers did the same, such as Christian Dior, who signed a new license with Kanebo in 1963, as well as Burberry with Sanyo Shokai (1969), Yves Saint Laurent with Kawabe (1970), and Courrèges with Itokin (1980).[16]

For companies that did not want to transfer their production to Japan—or could not, for legal reasons, like Swiss watchmakers—exporting through trading companies was the way to access the Japanese market. Trading companies were also linked to department stores, which were the main sales outlets for luxury goods in Japan until the 1990s. Thus, whatever the mode of entry (subsidiary, licensed production, or export), retailing depended on the same actor: the department stores. Chart 1.2 shows that sales of all Japanese department stores rose steadily between 1960 and 1991 (1995 if measured in dollars), with periods of acceleration in the early 1970s and the latter part of the 1980s. Measured in dollars, the period of the financial bubble, during which the yen was extremely strong, shows an impressive increase, from 28.6 billion sales in 1985 to 64.3 billion in 1990 and a peak of 91.2 billion in 1995. These figures highlight the importance of department stores and the Japanese market in general for European luxury brands. After the bubble burst in 1991, sales entered a phase of stagnation and decline (since 1996, if measured in dollars). Although these figures also include high-end domestic products, especially food—not only foreign luxury goods—sales of foreign luxury goods followed the general trend. The global financial crisis of 2008 had a strong negative impact, but the decline then stabilized owing to Chinese tourism—until the dramatic fall brought about by COVID-19.

However, the decline of department stores since the 1990s was not the only consequence of the slowdown of the Japanese economy. It also, and perhaps more importantly, reflects the changing role of these outlets in the Japanese luxury market. The

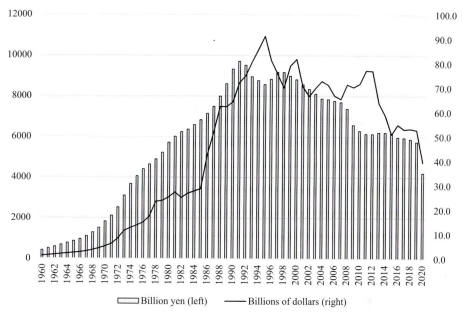

Chart 1.2 Sales of Japanese department stores, in billion yen and billion dollars, 1960–2020.
Source: *Nihon hyakatten kyokai tokei nenpo*, 1960–2020

liberalization of the 1990s allowed European luxury brands—themselves bought by conglomerates with the financial means to fulfil their ambitions—to reinforce their direct presence on the Japanese market. This presence was necessary for implementing the new strategy of creating and managing global brands, which implied strong control by the head offices and the development of a network of mono-brand stores (see Chapter 4). After 1990, most luxury brands opened subsidiaries in Japan: Coach (1991), Miu Miu (1991), Bulgari (1991), Giorgio Armani (1995), Vivienne Westwood (1996), Tag Heuer (1997), Burberry (2000), Paul Smith (2002), Berlutti (2002), Prada (2003), Cartier (2003), Bottega Veneta (2006), etc.[17] Their direct presence in Japan allowed them to control the extension of the retail network more effectively. These subsidiaries supervised the opening of mono-brand boutiques outside the department stores and ended the licensing contracts.

Christian Dior provides an excellent example.[18] This brand had long been established on the Japanese market, but it suffered from a blurred image owing to excessive diversification brought about by the multiplication of licenses. After its purchase by Bernard Arnault in 1984 and the foundation of LVMH in 1987, a new strategy saw the end of licenses for particular markets and the development of a global network of mono-brand stores. In Japan, the licensing contract with Kanebo was terminated in 1997. The French fashion house opened its own subsidiary, Christian Dior Japan, in 2003.[19] Its network of boutiques across the country grew from six shops in 2000 to nineteen in 2019.[20]

Burberry followed a similar trajectory.[21] In 2000, the British company's headquarters renegotiated its license agreement with Sanyo Shokai to strengthen its control over the

Figure 1.2 Chanel store, Ginza, Tokyo, 2015.
Source: Getty Image, ID: 462969094
Credit: Anadolu Agency / Contributor

Figure 1.3 Prada and Louis Vuitton stores in Shinsaibashi, Osaka, 2020.
Source: author

design of manufactured goods. In 2014, it finally terminated the license. In the same year, Burberry founded a sales subsidiary in Japan and opened a large mono-brand store in the Omotesando district of Tokyo.[22] Since 2000, it has not been a department store but a flagship store in luxury districts such as Ginza and Omotesando in Tokyo or Shinsaibashi in Osaka, which became the preferred mode of entry for brands not yet established in the Japanese archipelago. In the case of Fendi, LVMH launched its sales network in Japan with the opening of a mono-brand store in Tokyo in 2003.[23]

1.3 Accessing the Chinese market

Sales of European luxury goods in China were almost non-existent in the mid-1990s, but twenty-five years later, Chinese nationals accounted for between a third and a half of the global luxury market, depending on the type of product. More specifically, according to the consulting firm Bain & Co., China's share of global consumption of luxury consumer goods rose from 2 percent in 2000 to 35 percent in 2019. The growth was extraordinary and raised the question of the relationship between luxury brands and Chinese customers. It is in this context that the mode of entry to the Chinese market must be considered. Access to these consumers is not only direct, through points of sale established in the territory, but also indirect, thanks to sales in other countries, through Chinese tourists, and on the internet. Moreover, these contacts started mainly after the second half of the 1990s—that is, after the formation of the luxury conglomerates that transformed the luxury industry. The impact of the passage from a small family business with limited financial means to a listed multinational, essential for reorganizing a presence in Japan, is not observed in the Chinese case. Luxury groups with almost unlimited means and managing globalized brands imposed themselves on the Chinese luxury market when it opened. However, whereas these large companies, from 1990 onwards, benefited from a liberalized environment in Japan to redeploy, the situation is still different in China, where regulation remains strong. Moreover, the average Chinese consumer had little knowledge of Western luxury brands at the beginning of the twenty-first century. A process of education was necessary.[24]

In this context, the opening of mono-brand stores, particularly within the many luxury shopping centers that developed throughout the country, made perfect sense. The Swiss watch brand Omega illustrates this phenomenon. Although it opened after-sales service centers in Shanghai (1980) and Beijing (1985), it was only present through state-owned shops, which strictly controlled the import and sale of watches in the country until the 1990s. After 2000, it was a partnership between Swatch Group, owner of Omega, and the Chinese company Xinyu Hengdeli that enabled a network of boutiques. Hengdeli is a private company, listed on the Hong Kong Stock Exchange and founded by Zhang Yuping, a former employee of a state-owned watch distribution company. In the second half of the 1990s, he bought several watch distribution and retail companies in the context of the privatization of this sector. He quickly established himself as the largest watch retailer in China, with a network of stores that grew from sixty-five in 2005 to 482

Figure 1.4 Cooperation with Asian celebrities enables luxury brands to strengthen proximity with local customers. Hong Kong, 2015.
Source: author

in 2015. Hengdeli also worked with several hundred local distributors throughout China. In 2003, Swatch Group and Hengdeli founded a joint venture for distributing Omega watches in China, followed by a second one in 2007 for the licensed management of Omega boutiques. Finally, in 2010, Swatch took over 50 percent of the capital of a Hengdeli subsidiary that specialized in real estate investments. These various actions favored the expansion of Omega boutiques throughout the country, their number rising from eighty-four in 2010 to 150 in 2016.[25]

The example of Omega illustrates the challenge of real estate investment. European luxury goods stores began to appear in five-star hotels in the 1990s, before spreading to department stores in major Chinese cities and then to luxury shopping malls built across the country. They have become the main locations for the mono-brand stores of the big names in fashion and luxury. Francesca Bonetti's work on the expansion of Italian luxury brands in the Chinese market also shows that access to specialized shopping malls, as well as collaboration with local partners that have the means to manage a network of retailers (such as Hengdeli for Omega), is essential for success in China.[26] Luxury conglomerates have a clear competitive advantage in negotiating access to these large malls, both because they represent many brands and because they have the capital to invest directly in large projects. Thus, while the various Richemont brands negotiated their access to Chinese department stores individually until the early 2000s, the group then decided to centralize these negotiations to increase its negotiating power. Its subsidiary, Richemont Asia Pacific Ltd (Hong Kong), which works with various property tycoons in China, mainly carries out this task. In addition, in 2003, Richemont appointed British citizen Simon Murray, who made his fortune in finance and real estate in China and Southeast Asia, to its board of directors. LVMH pursues a similar but more ambitious strategy, marked by direct investments in certain real estate projects through its subsidiaries L Capital Asia (LCA, later renamed L Catterton Asia) and L Real Estate (LRE). For example, LCA signed an agreement in 2010 with the distributor Emperor Watch and Jewellery, one of the largest watch retailers in China after Hengdeli. As for LRE, it invested in several luxury shopping centers, notably in Shanghai.[27] These few examples highlight the link between the large multinational company and the ability to penetrate new markets. It should also be noted that the strategy deployed by Richemont and LVMH in China is not limited to China. It is also implemented in other emerging countries such as India, Singapore, and Malaysia.

Finally, the development of online sales of luxury goods (€1.3 billion in 2005 and 1 percent of the world market; €33.3 billion and 12 percent in 2019),[28] a phenomenon particularly marked in China, is based on a similar principle of collaboration between the major European groups and Chinese sales platforms. Thus, in 2018, the financial arm of LVMH, L Catterton Asia, announced a partnership with the Chinese e-commerce companies Secoo Holding and JD.com.[29] As for Richemont, it formed a partnership the same year with the giant Alibaba through its online sales subsidiary Yoox Net-a-Porter (YNAP).[30] Big business thus controls access to e-commerce for luxury goods in China as they do for physical distribution.

However, despite extremely strong growth, which attracts the attention of all luxury companies, China is characterized by a particularly high political risk. First of all, while the Chinese authorities had encouraged widespread enrichment during the 1990s and 2000s, the arrival of Xi Jinping at the head of the Chinese Communist Party (2012) and the People's Republic of China (2013) has led to a new and more uncertain context for luxury companies. Firstly, it has implemented an anti-corruption policy which has had negative effects on the consumption of certain goods, such as Swiss watches. Between 2012 and 2015, the value of Swiss watch exports to China fell by 19% and the average price of a watch by 35 percent.[31] Consumption patterns then changed, with luxury goods becoming personal consumption goods rather than objects of bribery, and the market has been on the rise again since 2016. Furthermore, in 2021, Xi Jinping launched a new campaign to reduce inequality, the slogan of which is "common prosperity." It represents a new threat to the consumption of luxury goods, although it is too early to measure its effects. Finally, let's highlight the particular case of Hong Kong, which had become during the 2000s a privileged place for luxury purchase tourism by Chinese nationals. Since 2014, the Umbrella Movement and the numerous democratic protests have had disastrous consequences for tourism and the sale of luxury goods. Between 2012 and 2018, Swiss watch exports to Hong Kong collapsed by 31 percent.[32] These various examples illustrate the challenge of political risk in the world's largest luxury market.

1.4 Democratization of luxury and globalization

The globalization of luxury markets is not only based on geographical expansion but also on expanding the sale of luxury goods to the middle classes—a process sometimes referred to as the democratization of luxury. Until the 1970s, the luxury industry concentrated in a niche market. Small, family-owned companies produced quality clothing, perfumes, watches, and accessories in limited editions for a small social elite. The consumption of luxury goods such as Chanel suits, Guerlain perfume, Bulgari jewelry, or Patek Philippe watches allowed for social distinction through conspicuous consumption, as economists and sociologists such as Thorstein Veblen, Georg Simmel, and Pierre Bourdieu have shown.[33]

However, the transformation of the luxury industry during the 1980s and 1990s was accompanied by a process of extending the offer through the production of specific goods (Louis Vuitton and Christian Dior accessories) or the launch of second brands (Emporio Armani) that were financially accessible to large sections of the population. The continuation of traditional activities in the field of creation (such as participation in haute couture shows or the design of watches with sophisticated complications) made it possible to maintain and reinforce the legitimacy of the brands as the embodiment of luxury while offering a strong added value in the form of less costly accessories that bore the designer's label.

The democratization of luxury has two main objectives. Firstly, the aim is to increase profits. The mass sale of accessories with a large profit margin—thanks to the combination of industrial production with a high value-added brand—ensures substantial revenues for luxury companies. Christian Dior SA was a forerunner at producing accessories under license around the world, ensuring high revenues during the 1970s. In 1977, for example, accessories accounted for 40.8 percent of the company's turnover but 70.2 percent of profits. Haute couture and ready-to-wear were loss-making but necessary to build a luxury brand that could sell accessories at comfortable margins.[34] Since the 1980s and 1990s, this business model has become a reference in the global luxury industry, especially for fashion brands.

Secondly, the democratization of luxury has further enhanced the reputation of a brand and extended the penetration of new markets. A case in point is Louis Vuitton, whose accessories, as mentioned above, helped popularize the brand on the Japanese market. Chandon sparkling wine is another example of this strategy. It dates back to the end of the 1950s, when the directors of the champagne house Moët & Chandon, the world's leading producer of champagne, decided to invest in the production of sparkling wine in Argentina, which they marketed under the Chandon brand. The experiment was extended in 1973 to Brazil and California, and later to Australia (1986). After the company was taken over by LVMH, it was applied to new emerging markets, such as China (2013) and India (2014).[35] This strategy made it possible to launch high-quality but cheap sparkling wines on the market, which introduced the product to new customers in the hope that they would switch to Moët & Chandon champagne in the future. The packaging of the two brands is similar, which makes it easy to transfer between the two brands.

Figure 1.5 Chandon sparkling wine made in Australia, Nara, Japan, 2020.
Source: author.

The democratization of luxury certainly makes it possible to increase profits in the short term, but it is not without danger. The profusion of a brand through multiple accessories can erode its image of exclusivity, which is precisely the basis of the luxury character. Some brands, such as Gucci, have lost their identity as luxury brands from poorly managing their expansion into accessories.[36] Authors such as Jean-Noël Kapferer and Vincent Bastien assert that democratization involves reducing social distance (notably, according to income level), while luxury involves precisely the opposite: it must create distance between the haves and have nots. The balance between the democratization of consumption and maintaining a classic luxury strategy is, therefore, difficult to achieve. A true luxury brand should not think it can maintain its exclusivity and attractiveness by extending its market.[37] However, in reality, most luxury companies adopt, more or less intensively, a democratization strategy. Danielle Allérès speaks of "accessible luxury" as opposed to "exclusive luxury."[38]

Despite this market expansion, one question remains open: what influence does the growing income inequality have on the growth of the luxury industry? Can we really talk about the democratization of luxury goods consumption? The work of the French economist Thomas Piketty has shown that inequality has increased worldwide since the 1980s.[39] For example, the share of national income going to the top 10 percent of the population has risen from less than 35 percent in the 1950s to 1980s to 45–50 percent in the 2000 to 2010 period for the United States.[40] The trend is similar in most countries of the world.[41] The transformation of the luxury industry is taking place precisely at a time when income inequality is entering a phase of rapid growth. Moreover, during 1994–2008, the luxury consumer goods market grew faster than the world economy as a whole, as discussed in the previous chapter (Chart 0.1). It is, therefore, not the increase in global GDP that leads almost mechanically to increases in the consumption of luxury goods. The relationship between social inequalities and the consumption of luxury goods has hardly ever been studied by historians and management researchers. They prefer to insist on the specificity of luxury goods (craftwork, quality materials, etc.), the hedonistic character of individualized consumers (the desire to please oneself by buying a luxury object) and the age of a manufacturing tradition—that is, elements that allow the consumption of luxury goods to be positively viewed and thus avoid the ideological debate on the significance of growing inequalities in contemporary societies. Moreover, the proximity between many social scientists and luxury companies is not conducive to adopting perspectives that the brands might perceive as unfavorable.[42] A few rare researchers in management have developed an original reflection aimed at showing how social inequality has favored the growth of the luxury industry (*critical luxury*).[43]

In this perspective, a recent study on wine exports worldwide between 2000 and 2018 has found a strong correlation between the value of wine exported and the level of inequality in importing countries.[44] The higher the income inequality in a country, the higher the consumption of expensive wine. This relationship has not diminished over the last two decades, which shows that the rise of the middle classes in emerging countries has not had a significant impact on this phenomenon. Similarly, champagne exports have risen sharply since the 1990s, along with increasing social inequality worldwide. Their value has risen from around $1.4 billion in 1995 to 1.5 billion in 2000 and 3.8 billion in 2018.[45] Thus, growth accelerated in the early twenty-first century. The countries that experienced the largest increase in champagne imports between 2000 and 2018 were those with the greatest income inequality (Chart 1.3).

The consumption of counterfeit goods is another ethical problem arising from the democratization of luxury goods. Although it is not possible to put an exact figure on this market, an OECD study estimated exports of counterfeit goods at $461 billion in 2013. More than half of these were luxury goods.[46] Management research has shown that a significant proportion of consumers of such goods are consciously buying them in order to own luxury brands. The democratization of luxury, which aims precisely at making these brands accessible to a mass of consumers, has thus a major impact on the development of counterfeiting.[47]

Luxury companies are not standing still in the face of this phenomenon. Some are intervening collectively, through trade associations, to pursue counterfeiters around the world. This is particularly true of the Federation of the Swiss watch industry.[48] In addition, some firms have recently started to use blockchain technology to guarantee the authenticity of their products. In 2021, LVMH, Cartier and Prada founded the Aura Blockchain Consortium.[49] Finally, the fight against counterfeiting is also being waged at the corporate level. At the end of the 2010s, LVMH employed several dozen lawyers specializing in this field.[50]

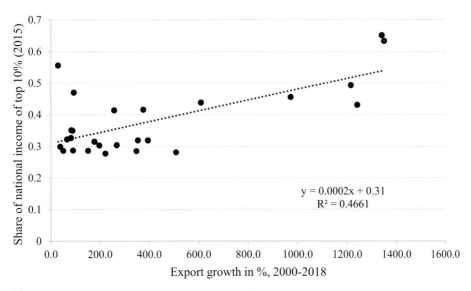

Chart 1.3 Champagne exports and income inequality.

Sources: World Inequality Database (https://wid.world/) and Comtrade.

Note: China (18th largest market in 2018) and the Czech Republic (29th) were eliminated due to extremely high growth rates (9,304 percent and 2,425 percent, respectively) that made the sample meaningless.

1.5 New consumption trends

The consumption of luxury goods had dramatically changed during the last fifteen years, beyond the globalization and the democratization of markets. The emergence of Millennials (generation born in 1980–95) and of Generation Z (1996–2010) as major consumers has a deep impact on luxury around the world. According to Bain & Co., generations born before 1980 represented 60 percent of the global consumption of luxury personal goods in 2020 but is expected to decrease to 25 percent in 2035.[51] These new consumers are much less attached to a traditional vision of luxury than their elders. As avid internet and social media users, they give importance to new ethical values such as sustainability, as well as racial and gender diversity. They are also less seduced by the classic image of luxury brands and desire products whose identity expresses their values. Louis Vuitton's transformation into a fashion brand, with the appointment of Marc Jacobs as artistic director in 1998, and then its collaboration with streetwear-inspired designers after 2015, in particular Virgil Abloh at the head of the men's collection, is an excellent illustration of how a classic luxury brand has managed to respond to the consumption desires of these new generations. All the major luxury fashion brands, from Chanel to Gucci and to Balenciaga have been deeply influenced by streetwear.

The increase in online sales is the best embodiment of these new trends. The global online personal goods market grew from €4.3 billion in 2010 to 33 billion in 2019.[52] It

Figure 1.6 Veuve Cliquot champagne, Schiphol Airport, Amsterdam, 2016.
Source: author.

was then boosted by the COVID-19 crisis: Bain & Co. estimates this market has doubled and reached 62 billion in 2021.[53] The share of online sales expanded hence from 2 percent in 2010 to 12 percent in 2019 and 22 percent in 2021. The acceleration of the transition from retail to digital platforms represents a profound structural change in the luxury industry. This change is accompanied by new consumption practices.

At first, the conscientious consumption of new generations has led luxury companies to develop various initiatives to guarantee the ethical origin of their supplies. For example, jewelers and watchmakers have helped to develop institutions that recognise that the gold and diamonds they use have been produced with respect for working conditions and the environment. Fairtrade and Fairmined Gold was one of the first ethical gold certification programs, launched in 2011 with the support of several brands, among which Chopard.[54] In addition, all major luxury companies have adopted various programs since the late 2010s to reduce their impact on climate change. In 2019, French President Emmanuel Macron has tasked François-Henri Pinault, CEO of Kering, with bringing together fashion brands—one of the most polluting industries after oil— around a Fashion Pact to take various measures to improve their environmental practices.[55] However, it remains difficult to measure the real usefulness of these measures, which are also akin to greenwashing to improve the image of companies and their brands.

Next, the desire of new generations to reduce their impact on the environment has also contributed to the inclusion of luxury in the circular economy. The burgeoning second-hand market for luxury goods is an excellent expression of this trend. According to Bain & Co., the luxury resale market grew from €17 billion in 2015 to 26 billion in 2019.[56] This represented about 10 percent of the luxury personal goods market in 2019. The growth of second-hand luxury relies on digital platforms, such as The RealReal, founded in 2011 in the US by IT entrepreneur Julie L. Wainwright. Listed in Nasdaq since 2019, this company reported sales of $137 million in 2017 and 468 million in 2021.[57] Conglomerates have realized that the second-hand sector has great growth potential. In 2018, the online watch reseller Watchfinder was acquired by Richemont, which owns Cartier. Three years later, in 2021, Kering took a stake in Vestiaire Collective, the world's largest second-hand platform for fashion.

The rising interest in experiential luxury, including travel, dining, and entertainment, is another expression of new consumption trends. In 2010–17, the market for luxury experiences (hospitality, cruises, and fine dining) showed a 10 percent growth rate and experience-based goods (fine art, luxury cars, private jets, and yachts) 9 percent, while luxury goods (cosmetics, fashion, jewelry, and watches) only 6 percent.[58] Here again, conglomerates demonstrated their ability to understand these new needs. For example, LVMH has invested in luxury hotels in 2006 with the launch of Cheval Blanc in Courchevel (2006) and founded LVMH Hotel Management (2010) to pursue the development of the concept. It acquired in 2019 the Belmond luxury hotels chain for $3.2 billion.[59] Moreover, in 2008, LVMH purchased the Dutch yacht manufacturer Royal Van Lent.[60] Finally, it should be noted that improving the online sales environment is currently one of the major challenges of experiential luxury.[61]

1.6 Conclusion

Since the 1980s and 1990s, the globalization of markets has transformed the European luxury goods industry. The strong growth in the Japanese market, followed by the opening of China, was accompanied by an acceleration of sales in emerging countries such as Russia and the nations of Southeast Asia. The consumption of luxury goods has become a global phenomenon based on a consumer profile that has changed significantly. The rich and super-rich remain the main target of luxury goods producers, of course, especially as their incomes are growing exponentially in the context of increasing social inequality in most countries. However, the launch of accessories and second brands has extended consumption to middle-class and even working-class women in what has been called the "democratization of luxury." However, if the globalization of markets has contributed to the birth of the modern luxury industry, the causal link is not an automatic one. Globalization is an opportunity seized by entrepreneurs to set up new business models that lead to increased sales and profits. The large multinational company is the dominant organizational form in this new market.

CHAPTER 2
THE DOMINANCE OF BIG BUSINESS

Since 1994, the French Ministry of Culture has awarded the title of "Master of Art" to honor independent craftsmen and encourage the perpetuation of French excellence in traditional skills. In 2006, it awarded the title for the first time to employees of multinational enterprises—the four heads of workshops belonging to famous luxury houses Baccarat, Chanel, Hermès and Louis Vuitton.[1]

The practice continues to this day, in collaboration with the Comité Colbert, an association bringing together the French luxury houses since 1954. Each year, Comité Colbert proposes a list of people to receive the honor. It is no longer just the independent craftsman, the bearer of know-how or the manager of a small business who is honored, but the craftsman-employee, whose know-how is one of the essential resources for the international competitiveness of large companies listed on the stock exchange.

The permanence of authentic know-how lies at the heart of the communication strategy of the major luxury companies, such as LVMH, Swatch Group, and Richemont, which present themselves as the guarantors of the transmission of a craft tradition to future generations.[2] However, although the discourse and practice of the major players in the luxury industry insist on the maintenance and historical continuity of European artisanal excellence, the organizational structure of the luxury industry underwent a profound upheaval in the 1980s and 1990s. Up until then, small, independent, family-run businesses dominated the industry. After then, multinational, publicly traded companies took over. The growth in turnover of some of the most famous brands between the 1970s and the present is emblematic of this change. The turnover of Rolex, for example, rose from around 190 million Swiss francs in 1979 ($114 million) to 5.7 billion in 2017 ($5.8 billion).[3] As for Christian Dior Couture, it amounted to €26 million (169 million FF) in 1977 and more than €1.8 billion in 2015–16.[4] Finally, Giorgio Armani saw its sales soar, from nearly €500,000 in 1978 to 2.7 billion in 2015.[5] These examples illustrate the change in scale that the European luxury industry was undergoing at the end of the twentieth century.

The absence of aggregate data at the level of the entire luxury industry makes it hard to give an accurate general analysis of the transformation of the sector. The chapters in the second part of this book deal with the specific case of conglomerates and other organizational modes adopted by luxury companies. However, there is no global census. For France, the cumulative turnover of all the members of the Comité Colbert rose from €4.1 billion in 1984 to 39.6 billion in 2013.[6] It increased tenfold in thirty years.

The contemporary luxury industry is, therefore, the result of a process of structural transformation that took place at the end of the twentieth century. To analyze it here, let us use the ranking of the 100 largest luxury companies published annually by the consulting firm Deloitte. The use of such a document requires a preliminary remark, as it directly influences the discourse on the luxury industry in this book. Firstly, the authors do not define what luxury is. They include several companies that produce fashion accessories rather than luxury itself, such as the American watch group Fossil and the Japanese clothing manufacturers Onward and Sanyo Shokai. However, these cases are exceptions. Therefore, while the figures quoted in this chapter should be considered more broad trends than an accurate reflection of reality, the Deloitte ranking is still usable for analyzing the luxury industry. Secondly, this ranking focuses on consumer goods. In particular, it excludes the hotel and automotive sectors, both of which are included in the study of organizational modes proposed in Part II. At the time of writing, the most recent version of the Deloitte ranking was the one published in 2019, based on turnover for the financial year 2017.[7] Table 2.1 shows the main characteristics of these companies.

2.1 A key resource: money

The year of the foundation of a luxury company is generally considered essential information. It lies at the heart of a brand's communication strategies because it allows them to insist on the long-term nature of their craft tradition and thus legitimizes their capacity to produce luxury. In its annual report, LVMH presents its portfolio of brands according to the chronology of their foundation, from its Clos des Lambrays vineyard (1365) to the fashion house created by the singer Rihanna (2017).[8] The age of luxury companies can also be seen in the ranking of the 100 largest companies today. They are, on average, seventy-two years old, and more than a quarter of them are more than 100 years old (twenty-six in total), the oldest being Hermès and Tiffany, both founded in 1837. Only five companies were established in the twenty-first century, including three jewelers from emerging countries. Furthermore, there is a significant correlation between the age of the company and its size. The largest luxury companies today are also the oldest (Table 2.2). The twenty largest in the world are, on average, 93.6 years old, compared to 60.2 years for the twenty smallest in the top 100. This ranking, therefore, seems to embody the timelessness of luxury and the competitiveness of brands with a long history.

Another reading of the competitiveness of these firms, which is not the one proposed by the marketing departments, is also possible. The world's largest luxury companies have a strong tendency to be listed on the stock exchange. The rate of listing even decreases gradually with the decrease in the size of the companies. For example, eighteen of the twenty largest companies are listed on the stock exchange, while only five of the twenty smallest are (Table 2.2). What does a company's presence in the financial markets mean? For its owners, it is a means of rapid personal enrichment. However, opening up the capital also has a function in the management of the company. It is essentially a matter of increasing the capital available to allow the company to grow rapidly. The new money is, of course, used to buy new brands and expand the portfolio, but also to develop

Table 2.1 The world's top 100 luxury companies, 2017

Rank	Name	Country	Sales of luxury goods, $ million	Share of the top 100 in %	Main activity	Foundation	Stock exchange listing
1	LVMH Moët Hennessy–Louis Vuitton SE	France	27 995	11,3	Diversified	1987	1987
2	The Estée Lauder Companies Inc.	United States	13 683	5,5	Cosmetics	1946	1995
3	Compagnie Financière Richemont SA	Switzerland	12 819	5,2	Watchmaking	1988	1988
4	Kering SA	France	12 168	4,9	Diversified	1963	1988
5	Luxottica Group SpA	Italy	10 322	4,2	Eyewear	1961	1990
6	Chanel	France	9 623	3,9	Fashion	1954	Unlisted
7	L'Oréal Luxe	France	9 549	3,9	Cosmetics	1909	1963
8	The Swatch Group Ltd	Switzerland	7 819	3,2	Watchmaking	1983	1983
9	Chow Tai Fook Jewellery Group	Hong Kong	7 575	3,1	Jewelry	1929	2011
10	PVH Corp.	United States	7 355	3,0	Fashion	1881	1920
11	Hermès International SCA	France	6 255	2,5	Leather goods	1837	1993
12	Ralph Lauren Co.	United States	6 182	2,5	Fashion	1967	1997
13	Tapestry, Inc. (formerly Coach, Inc.)	United States	5 880	2,4	Fashion	1941	2000
14	Rolex SA	Switzerland	5 686	2,3	Watchmaking	1905	Unlisted
15	Lao Feng Xiang Co, Ltd	China	5 346	2,2	jewellery	1848	1992
16	Shiseido Prestige & Fragrance	Japan	4 748	1,9	Cosmetics	1872	1949
17	Michael Kors Holdings	United States	4 719	1,9	Fashion	1981	2011

(Continued)

Table 2.1 (*Continued*)

Rank	Name	Country	Sales of luxury goods, $ million	Share of the top 100 in %	Main activity	Foundation	Stock exchange listing
18	Tiffany & Co	United States	4 170	1,7	Jewelry	1837	1987
19	Burberry Group plc	Great Britain	3 619	1,5	Fashion	1856	2002
20	Pandora	Denmark	3 452	1,4	Jewelry	1982	2010
21	Prada Group	Italy	3 445	1,4	Fashion	1913	2011
22	Coty Luxury	United States	3 211	1,3	Perfumery	1904	2013
23	Hugo Boss AG	Germany	3 080	1,2	Fashion	1924	1985
24	Swarovski Crystal	Austria	3 043	1,2	Jewelry	1895	Unlisted
25	Fossil Group	United States	2 683	1,1	Watchmaking	1984	1993
26	Giorgio Armani SpA	Italy	2 637	1,1	Fashion	1975	Unlisted
27	Titan Company	India	2 449	1,0	Jewelry	1984	2000
28	Puig S.L.	Spain	2 181	0,9	Cosmetics	1911	Unlisted
29	Kosé Corporation	Japan	2 071	0,8	Cosmetics	1946	1999
30	Chow Sang Sang Holdings	Hong Kong	1 863	0,8	Jewelry	1934	1973
31	Max Mara Fashion Group Srl	Italy	1 784	0,7	Fashion	1951	Unlisted
32	Luk Fook Holdings	Hong Kong	1 777	0,7	Jewelry	1991	1997
33	OTB SpA	Italy	1 713	0,7	Fashion	1978	Unlisted
34	Onward Holdings Co. Ltd	Japan	1 670	0,7	Fashion	1927	1960

	Company	Country	Revenue	Share	Sector	Founded	Listed
35	Kalyan Jewellers India Pvt. Limited	India	1 628	0,7	Jewelry	1993	Unlisted
36	Salvatore Ferragamo SpA	Italy	1 556	0,6	Shoes	1927	2011
37	Pola Orbis Holdings Inc.	Japan	1 552	0,6	Cosmetics	1929	2010
38	L'Occitane International SA	Luxembourg	1 541	0,6	Cosmetics	1976	2010
39	Dolce & Gabbana	Italy	1 515	0,6	Fashion	1985	Unlisted
40	PC Jeweller	India	1 490	0,6	Jewelry	2005	2012
41	Valentino SpA	Italy	1 380	0,6	Fashion	1960	Unlisted
42	Eastern Gold Jade Co.	China	1 372	0,6	Jewelry	1993	1997
43	Ermenegildo Zegna Holditalia	Italy	1 369	0,6	Fashion	1910	Unlisted
44	Moncler SpA	Italy	1 345	0,5	Fashion	1952	2013
45	Patek Philippe SA	Switzerland	1 239	0,5	Watchmaking	1839	Unlisted
46	Safilo Group	Italy	1 180	0,5	Eyewear	1934	2005
47	Joyalukkas India	India	1 141	0,5	Jewelry	2009	Unlisted
48	Tod's SpA	Italy	1 108	0,4	Shoes	1978	2000
49	Tory Burch	United States	1 050	0,4	Fashion	2004	Unlisted
50	SMPC SAS	France	1 128	0,5	Fashion	1984	2017
51	Audemars Piguet	Switzerland	995	0,4	Watchmaking	1875	Unlisted
52	Revlon Inc.	United States	953	0,4	Cosmetics	1932	1996
53	Chopard & Cie	Switzerland	848	0,3	Watchmaking	1860	Unlisted
54	Ted Baker	Great Britain	769	0,3	Fashion	1988	2001

(Continued)

Table 2.1 *(Continued)*

Rank	Name	Country	Sales of luxury goods, $ million	Share of the top 100 in %	Main activity	Foundation	Stock exchange listing
55	Gianni Versace	Italy	760	0,3	Fashion	1978	Unlisted
56	Graff Diamonds International	Great Britain	693	0,3	Jewelry	1960	Unlisted
57	Samsonite International (Tumi brand)	United States	678	0,3	Travel articles	1910	2011
58	Longchamp	France	626	0,3	Leather goods	1948	Unlisted
59	Cole Haan	United States	600	0,2	Shoes	1928	Unlisted
60	Inter Parfums	United States	591	0,2	Perfumery	1985	1988
61	Furla SpA	Italy	574	0,2	Leather goods	1927	Unlisted
62	Brunello Cucinelli SpA	Italy	570	0,2	Fashion	1978	2012
63	Movado Group, Inc.	United States	568	0,2	Watchmaking	1881	1993
64	Gerhard D. Wempe KG	Germany	565	0,2	Watchmaking (distribution)	1878	Unlisted
65	Chow Tai Seng Jewellery Co. Ltd	China	563	0,2	Jewelry	2007	2017
66	Sanyo Shokai	Japan	558	0,2	Fashion	1943	1971
67	Zhejiang Ming Jewellery Co.	China	545	0,2	Jewelry	1987	2012
68	Marcolin Group	Italy	529	0,2	Eyewear	1961	Unlisted
69	Tse Sui Luen Jewellery	Hong Kong	489	0,2	Jewelry	1971	1987
70	De Rigo SpA	Italy	483	0,2	Eyewear	1978	1995
71	Marc O'Polo AG	Germany	466	0,2	Fashion	1968	Unlisted

	Company	Country			Sector		
72	Canada Goose Holdings	Canada	461	0,2	Outdoor clothing	1957	2017
73	Vera Bradley Inc.	United States	455	0,2	Travel articles	1982	2010
74	Breitling SA	Switzerland	437	0,2	Watchmaking	1884	Unlisted
75	Kurt Geiger	Great Britain	422	0,2	Shoes	1963	Unlisted
76	S Tous SL	Spain	415	0,2	Fashion (distribution)	1920	Unlisted
77	Euroitalia	Italy	402	0,2	Perfumery	1978	Unlisted
78	Zadig & Voltaire	France	394	0,2	Fashion	1997	Unlisted
79	Restoque	Brazil	391	0,2	Fashion (distribution)	1982	2008
80	Sociedad Textil Lonia	Spain	389	0,2	Fashion	1997	Unlisted
81	Liu Jo	Italy	388	0,2	Fashion	1995	Unlisted
82	Aeffe	Italy	357	0,1	Fashion	1972	2007
83	Etro SpA	Italy	338	0,1	Fashion	1968	Unlisted
84	Franck Muller Group	Switzerland	305	0,1	Watchmaking	1991	Unlisted
85	Marc Cain Holding	Germany	296	0,1	Fashion	1973	Unlisted
86	Twinset – Simona Berbieri	Italy	287	0,1	Fashion	1987	Unlisted
87	Tribhovandas Bhimji Zaveri	India	273	0,1	Jewelry	1864	2011
88	J. Barbour & Sons	Great Britain	270	0,1	Fashion	1894	Unlisted
89	Festina Lotus SA	Spain	268	0,1	Watchmaking	1984	Unlisted

(Continued)

Table 2.1 (*Continued*)

Rank	Name	Country	Sales of luxury goods, $ million	Share of the top 100 in %	Main activity	Foundation	Stock exchange listing
90	Richard Mille SA	Switzerland	264	0,1	Watchmaking	2001	Unlisted
91	Fashion Box SpA	Italy	262	0,1	Fashion	1981	Unlisted
92	Falke KGaA	Germany	262	0,1	Fashion	1895	Unlisted
93	Charles Tyrwhitt Shirts Limited	Great Britain	250	0,1	Fashion	1986	Unlisted
94	Van de Velde NV	Belgium	235	0,1	Lingerie	1919	1997
95	Paul Smith Group	Great Britain	234	0,1	Fashion	1970	Unlisted
96	Giuseppe Zanotti SpA	Italy	232	0,1	Diversified	1990	Unlisted
97	K. Mikimoto & Co. Ltd	Japan	226	0,1	Jewelry	1899	Unlisted
98	Mulberry Group	Great Britain	225	0,1	Fashion	1971	2008
99	Acne Studios Holding AB	Sweden	222	0,1	Fashion	1996	Unlisted
100	Trinity Limited	Hong Kong	218	0,1	Fashion	ca.1960	2009

Source: Deloitte 2019; listing dates added by the author based on annual reports and the *International Directory of Company Histories* series, 150 volumes, Farmington Hills: St. James Press, 1988–2014.

Table 2.2 Average age and stock market listing of luxury companies by size, 2017

Rank	1–20	21–40	41–60	61–80	81–100
Average age	93.6	68.4	73.7	63.1	60.2
Listed companies (N)	18	13	9	10	5

Source: See Table 2.1.

the network of boutiques on which the global expansion of luxury brands is based. Money becomes the resource that ensures a presence in the only market that matters now: the global market.

However, the date of the initial public offering (IPO) says as much about the state of competitiveness of luxury companies as it does about their foundation. This is a far cry from the discourse on the timelessness and permanence of luxury, which is linked to their ancient historical roots. Of the fifty-five luxury companies listed on the stock exchange in 2017, only four went public before 1970. The first are two Japanese companies that had no connection with the luxury sector at the time and whose entry into the luxury market is recent: the cosmetics manufacturer Shiseido and the clothing producer Onward. The third firm is the French cosmetics and perfume manufacturer L'Oréal, a family-owned company founded in 1909 that transformed into a multinational company with a strong presence in the luxury sector when it was listed on the stock exchange in 1963. Two years later, in 1965, it took over Lancôme perfumes, acquired half of the capital of the haute couture house Courrèges and signed a licensing agreement with the couturier Guy Laroche for the production of perfumes. L'Oréal continued to grow through acquisitions and licensing agreements and, in the mid-1980s, became the world's largest cosmetics company.[9] Finally, the American fashion group Phillips Van Heusen was listed on the New York Stock Exchange in 1920. Two other companies followed suit in the 1970s: Japanese clothing manufacturer Sanyo Shokai, shortly after signing a license to produce Burberry coats (1971), and Hong Kong jewelry distributor Chow Sang Sang Holdings (1973). It was mainly the expansion of the distribution network and the reorganization of the groups that required the injection of capital. However, the major changes took place over the following decades: eight companies went public in the 1980s, thirteen in the 1990s, nine in the 2000s, and eighteen between 2010 and 2017. Hence, the transition of the luxury industry to financial capitalism is a recent phenomenon and a major characteristic of the sector.

It should be noted, however, that not all unlisted companies are small, family-run businesses that pursue sustainable development. Some of them are owned by investment funds that inject cash into these firms to ensure their growth on the global market before selling them for prodigious profits. The Italian haute couture house Valentino, for example, has been owned since 2012 by the Qatari fund Mayhoola for Investments SPC;[10] the Swiss watchmaker Breitling is controlled by CVC Capital Partners;[11] the Apax Partners fund owns the American shoe manufacturer Cole Haan.[12] LVMH also has its own investment company, Luxury Ventures, which carries out similar operations.

Figure 2.1 The cooperation with the Chinese film industry allows Breitling to strengthen its presence in the Asian markets at the beginning of the twenty-first century.
Source: *Europa Star*, vol. 246, 2001, p. 256. © Archives Europa Star.

2.2 The dominance of European societies

The second striking feature of the luxury industry is the dominance of European companies. Seventy-four of the world's top 100 luxury companies have their headquarters in Europe. However, they account for only 65.8 percent of the combined turnover of the top 100. Therefore, European companies are, on average, smaller than non-European companies. This result may be surprising, given that the world's largest luxury company, LVMH, is French, and the Richemont (no. 3) and Kering (no. 4) groups are also based in Europe. This apparent contradiction is explained by the over-representation of European companies among the smaller firms (thirty-five of the fifty companies with a turnover of under $1 billion in 2017).

In addition, many non-European luxury companies have European brands in their portfolio. US cosmetics maker Estée Lauder (no. 2) owns some thirty brands, including Jo Malone London, Ermenegildo Zegna, and Kilian Paris perfumes. Its Japanese competitor Shiseido (no. 16), which has developed on the basis of its own brands, has held the license for Dolce & Gabbana since 2016. As for the American watchmaker Movado (no. 63), it owns the Swiss watch brand Ebel. Finally, the Hong Kong group Trinity (no. 100) moved from textile production to fashion by buying the British tailor Kent & Curwen (2008) and the Italian designer Cerruti 1881 (2011). However, not all non-European companies follow this model. This is particularly true of American fashion retailers and Asian jewelers, which have remained firmly rooted in their respective markets. It is, therefore, not imperative to own European brands to appear in the top 100 luxury companies.

Of the seventy-four European companies, France is overwhelmingly dominant in terms of turnover (8 companies; 27.5 percent of the total turnover of the top 100), and Italy (24; 14 percent), Switzerland (9; 12.3 percent) and Great Britain (9; 4.5 percent) in terms of the number of companies. Therefore, the European luxury goods industry is essentially based in four countries, which account for 50 percent of the companies and more than 58 percent of the total turnover. Germany (5; 1.9 percent), Austria (1; 1.2 percent), Belgium (1; 0.2 percent), Denmark (1; 1.4 percent), Spain (4; 1.3 percent), Luxembourg (1; 1.6 percent), and Sweden (1; 0.1 percent) follow.

Figure 2.2 Kent & Curven store, Hong Kong, 2020.
Source: Wikimedia Commons
https://commons.wikimedia.org/wiki/File:HK_%E9%87%91%E9%90%98_Admiralty_%E9%87%91%E9%90
%98%E9%81%93_Queensway_%E5%A4%AA%E5%8F%A4%E5%BB%A3%E5%A0%B4_Pacific_Place_
mall_shop_Kent_%26_Curwen_clothing_May_2020_SS2_05.jpg?uselang=fr

Outside Europe, the luxury goods industry is also concentrated in about ten countries. These are mainly the United States (14 companies; 19.5 percent of turnover), Japan (6; 4.4 percent), China/Hong Kong (9; 8 percent), and India (5; 2.8 percent). Apart from some US companies, these are mainly companies with little presence in foreign markets and whose growth is mainly based on a large domestic market. Their presence among the representatives of a global luxury industry is, therefore, questionable. Their brands are generally unknown to consumers in other countries, and their products are sold through distribution systems aimed at the domestic population. The case of Asian jewelry is emblematic of this situation.[13]

2.3 Sectoral and national specialization

Finally, the third characteristic of the modern luxury industry is the strong tendency for companies to specialize. With the notable exception of the two French conglomerates LVMH and Kering, which are active in a wide variety of sectors,[14] luxury companies tend to focus on one particular sector. The most important are as follows: fashion (40 companies), jewelry (18), watches (13), and cosmetics (8). These four sectors account for almost 80 percent of luxury companies.

Moreover, specialization is often accompanied by strong national roots. Most watch companies are Swiss, while jewelers are mostly Chinese or Indian, shoe and eyewear manufacturers are Italian, and perfume companies are American. Fashion is the only sector that transcends borders: although Italian and British companies are the most numerous, they can be found in many other European countries, as well as in Brazil, the United States, and Asia. The national dimension of several luxury sectors is not the only reflection of traditional know-how embedded in particular territories. Research on technology transfer shows that knowledge circulates on a global scale and is developed where companies need it.[15] For the luxury industry, the territorial anchoring of manufacturing traditions remains a major characteristic because it gives a definite competitive advantage to the companies that benefit from it. The safeguarding, maintenance, and transmission of technical skills in specific national spaces must be understood in the context of the construction of a brand's heritage.[16] The luxury industry invests in training and succession programs to perpetuate know-how, with the aim of making this heritage part of their marketing strategy. The real part of the artisanal gesture in the production of luxury goods is a highly sensitive subject that has never been studied in-depth.

It is also worth noting that in some cases an institutional framework influences the continuation of a local or national manufacturing tradition. For example, the Fédération de la Haute Couture et de la Mode, whose origins date back to the middle of the nineteenth century, sets the rules for entry as an haute couture house. These rules have the effect of keeping creative activities within the city of Paris, ensuring Paris remains the world capital of fashion.[17] Similarly, the Swiss watch industry has benefited since 1971 from legislation regulating the use of the *Swiss Made* label to keep a significant part of the

Figure 2.3 The Federation of the Swiss Watch Industry is actively engaged in the fight against counterfeiting, as illustrated by this operation to destroy fake watches with a steamroller, Wimmis (Switzerland), February 23, 2021.
Source: © Federation of the Swiss Watch Industry

production of watches on Swiss territory.[18] The establishment of a legal framework for protected designations of origin is not specific to the luxury industry.[19] However, the luxury industry benefits from it because it has transformed territorial anchoring into a marketing resource.

The specialization of most luxury companies does not mean that the brands they own are, for the most part, concentrated on one specific type of goods. Product diversification is a common phenomenon, but it is often undertaken by partner companies—except for the conglomerates LVMH and Kering, which carry out some diversification internally.[20] Between the 1950s and 1980s, it was mainly through licensing agreements that luxury companies, particularly the Parisian haute couture houses, developed their product range. Christian Dior and Pierre Cardin are excellent examples. While the parent company remained focused on fashion design, it signed dozens of contracts with partner companies to bring a multitude of accessories to the market. This approach has been significantly reformed since the 1990s, with a shift to stronger control by head offices, but the practice of licensed production has not disappeared.[21] The development of subcontracting for accessories largely explains the current specialization of luxury companies. Some companies use their competitive advantage in product development to offer accessories to fashion companies. This is the case for many cosmetics and perfume manufacturers, as well as some firms specializing in the licensed manufacture of watches or sunglasses.[22] Fossil, for example, produces watches for Armani and Michel Kors, while Luxottica manufactures glasses for Chanel and Tiffany. The mastery of specific know-how has thus enabled groups to develop a presence in the luxury sector while remaining active in other segments.[23]

Finally, luxury manufacturers have little involvement in markets other than the luxury market. According to Deloitte data, the combined luxury sales of the world's top 100 companies in 2017 represented 89.3 percent of their total revenue. Only sixteen companies are also active outside of luxury. These are mainly LVMH and Kering, two diversified conglomerates, as well as Japanese cosmetics manufacturers and some fashion companies that own consumer product lines.

2.4 Conclusion

An analysis of the global luxury industry based on the Deloitte census of the world's top 100 companies in 2017 provides a general picture of this sector at the beginning of the twenty-first century. Its main characteristics are as follows: the recent nature of the industry, in the sense that it is largely made up of new companies, although they manage old brands; its high concentration in a few dominant companies; a strong European base (especially, French, English, Italian, and Swiss); and a marked tendency towards specialization of activities.

Finally, there is the question of the profitability of the large European company. The luxury industry has a reputation for generating big profits. Which companies had the

Table 2.3 Profit rates by company size, 2017

Profit rate	>10%	5–10%	0–5%	<0%	Unknown
Number of companies	21	26	20	10	23
Average rate	15.3%	7.70%	2.37%	-7.50%	–
Average sales of luxury goods (million dollars)	5 001.5	2 755	1 279.7	642,1	1 660.6

Source: See Table 2.1.

Note: The profit rate is the net profit to turnover ratio.

highest margins in 2017? Owing to the private nature of many companies, Deloitte has only assessed the profit rate of seventy-seven companies. There is a very strong correlation between profit rate and company size (Table 2.3). The larger a luxury company is, the higher its profit rate. These companies are usually listed on the stock exchange, so high profits are their main objective.

CHAPTER 3
NEW MARKETING STRATEGIES BASED ON BRAND HERITAGE

In 2018, Cartier had an estimated turnover of over €5.3 billion, making it one of the world's leading jewelry brands. In addition, around 30 percent of its sales came from watches, with Cartier becoming the third-largest watch brand in the world behind Rolex and Omega.[1] Yet until the 1960s, the Parisian jeweler was still a small, family-run company producing jewelry and accessories for the aristocracy and upper-middle classes. How was such a company able to establish itself as one of the leaders in the global luxury goods industry within a few decades? Clearly, its takeover by the South African tycoon Anton Rupert and its integration into the Compagnie Financière Richemont in 1988 were decisive steps because they provided the capital needed to expand the production system and the sales network around the world. However, Cartier's success was not just a question of money. It was based primarily on a profound transformation of the brand, which allowed the sale of mass-produced accessories as luxury goods. Except for a few unique pieces of jewelry, which continued Cartier's tradition of excellence in the field of jewelry, the company's sales were largely based on iconic products such as Love rings and bracelets, Trinity wedding rings, and the Tank and Ballon Bleu watch collections.

The proliferation of accessories was certainly not a new phenomenon. Cartier had already launched various watch models at the beginning of the twentieth century, in collaboration with Swiss watch manufacturers. The Santos watch was produced for the first time in 1904, followed by the Tank model in 1918. However, until the 1960s, accessories represented only an auxiliary part of a production that remained focused on classic jewelry.[2] It was the continuation of this traditional positioning that limited the firm's profitability and growth at the end of the 1960s.[3]

In 1972, a group of investors and managers, led by Joseph Kanoui and Alain-Dominique Perrin, took over the business. Their main strategic choice was to reposition Cartier as an accessible luxury brand with the "Must de Cartier" concept (1973). The launch of accessories such as lighters, produced under license since 1968 by a company run by Perrin, and watches enabled a broadening of the customer base and a sharp increase in profits. The Santos and Tank watches were relaunched in the 1970s, accompanied by storytelling that gradually reinforced the brand's position as a watch manufacturer. They became one of the jeweler's new iconic products. The destruction of counterfeit Cartier watches in front of the international press was also staged to assert the brand's watchmaking image.[4]

The takeover by Richemont thus provided fresh capital to develop a marketing strategy in the early 1970s that consisted of building a strong brand based on the perpetuation of a tradition. Of course, at the beginning of the twenty-first century,

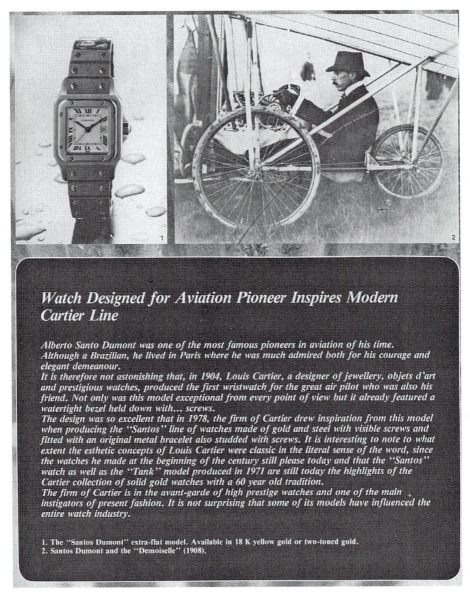

Figure 3.1 Advertisement for Cartier, 1981.

Source: *Eastern Jeweller and Watchmaker*, no. 183, 1981. © Archives Europa Star.

Cartier was an industrial company that mass-produced and sold goods that intrinsically had little to do with the creations of the first part of the twentieth century. However, the genius of the new marketing strategy implemented in the luxury industry since the 1980s consisted precisely in inscribing contemporary industrial production in a narrative that expressed the permanence of a tradition. This tradition was based on the selection of a certain number of iconic products (the Tank watch), symbols (the panther), messages

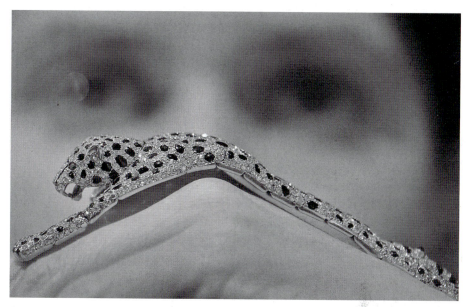

Figure 3.2 A symbol of femininity, sensuality, and independence, the panther has been used by Jeanne Toussaint in her creations for Cartier since the interwar period, as in this bracelet made in 1952 for the Duchess of Windsor. It has become the symbol of the jeweler.
Source: Getty Image, ID: 104375710
Credit: Peter Macdiarmid / Staff

("Cartier, jeweller of kings, king of jewellers") and personalities from Cartier's history (Jeanne Toussaint, friend of Coco Chanel, lover of Louis Cartier, and artistic director of the jeweler). These iconic products constituted the brand's *heritage*—some managers speak of its DNA. It is on this new concept that the modern luxury brands have been rebuilt to conquer the global market.

3.1 History, heritage, and storytelling

The modern luxury industry bases itself on stories and objects. Stories are the discursive basis for the attraction of brands, while objects are material embodiments of these narratives that help create value. The interaction between stories and objects is made possible by constructing a back story for the brand: a "heritage."

Brand management is not a new strategy in the luxury industry. As with other consumer goods, it dates back to the end of the nineteenth century, in the context of the industrialization of production and the expansion of distribution networks.[5] Once companies adopt brands, brand management becomes essential. However, the majorchange in the luxury industry in the 1980s and 1990s was the use of the past as a marketing resource. Luxury brands are now the heirs and keepers of a historical tradition, and this continuity legitimizes much of their positioning in luxury.

Management researchers have developed the concept of *brand heritage* to show how companies introduce historical elements into their brand management and how this process adds value.[6] A team of Swedish academics defines brand heritage as:

> a dimension of a brand's identity found in its track record, longevity, core values, use of symbols, and particularly in an organisational belief that its history is important.[7]

Thus, the notion of heritage is based on an objectivist view of history.[8] As a result, most of the work in luxury brand management has been carried out from a purely applied perspective to help business leaders identify and manage their heritage.

However, it is worth remembering a fundamental truth: history, as an embodiment of the past, does not exist as such. It is only a social construction depending on the observer.[9] Thus, heritage should not be seen as an accurate expression of the past but as an invented tradition, to use the famous words of British historians Eric Hobsbawm and Terence Ranger.[10] It represents a constructed narrative that includes various elements more or less strongly linked to the past. Luxury management gurus Jean-Noël Kapferer and Vincent Bastien state that:

> what is important is not simply the history, but the myth that can be created around it, the source of the brand's social idealization [. . .]. If there is no history, it must be invented.[11]

The narrative techniques used to build a legacy and manage a brand on this basis are called storytelling. Telling stories to engage audiences is a technique conceptualized and developed in American politics in the 1980s before being introduced into other fields, including management.[12] In the luxury industry, storytelling accompanies the building of evocative images and stories for global brands.

Chart 3.1 illustrates the relationship between the three concepts of history, heritage and storytelling in brand management. The history of a company, a brand or a creator belongs to the past. It includes a wide variety of facts that can only be partially brought to light and interpreted through the use of available sources (archives, products, testimonials, etc.). To build their brand identity, companies select a limited number of elements from their history and combine them with imaginary elements to make their heritage. Brand managers commonly refer to these various elements as the DNA of brands. The work of anthropologists Claude Lévi-Strauss and Bernard Crettaz on cultural identities shed a bright light on this process of building heritage. Crettaz, in particular, developed the concept of "bricolage" (tinkering) to show how identities are based on a combination of out-of-context elements drawn from the distant past and latter-day elements to give meaning to a present cultural identity.[13]

In the luxury industry, heritage is a marketing resource that requires specific management and allows three main actions to be coordinated: product development (which must materially embody the brand's heritage through, for example, the perpetuation

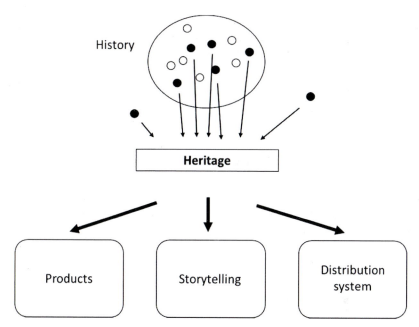

Chart 3.1 History, heritage, and storytelling in brand management.
Source: Author.

of iconic products), storytelling (what companies say about themselves in the media, museums and events in which they participate), and distribution (staging of the brand's products in shops and customer experience). The distinction between history, heritage, and storytelling allows us to go beyond the objectivist approach of management researchers to renew our understanding of how luxury companies manage the past as a resource.

European luxury companies adopted a new heritage-based branding strategy in the context of their organizational change and global expansion during the 1980s and 1990s. This strategy allowed them to have strong brand identities and offer consumers around the world a consistent set of products and narratives. It was made all the more necessary by most luxury companies no longer addressing the niche market of the super-rich but much larger social groups that included the middle classes. Mass communication had become indispensable. By asserting the continuity of a craft manufacturing tradition, heritage helps overcome the contradictions of luxury industrialization and maintains a high added value to products. The following section analyses how haute couture house Christian Dior implemented its new brand strategy based on heritage.[14]

3.2 The rise of a luxury brand in the global market: Christian Dior

Dior is now one of the most valuable luxury brands. In 2017, it was one of six fashion brands in the Interbrand ranking of the world's top 100 brands, alongside Louis Vuitton, Hermès, Gucci, Burberry, and Prada.[15] Until that year, the management of the Dior brand was divided between two companies. Christian Dior Couture SA controlled fashion products and all accessories except perfumes and cosmetics, which were managed by Parfums Christian Dior. Both companies were actually integrated into the LVMH conglomerate, the first as a subsidiary of the financial company that was LVMH's main shareholder and the second as a subsidiary of LVMH.[16] This distinction is important because the figures published by Christian Dior Couture (CDC)—the only ones available since 1987—do not include perfumes or cosmetics. The group's organization was simplified in 2017 after the takeover by LVMH, but no figures for this brand are published anymore.

CDC has experienced tremendous growth since the early 1990s, illustrating the transformation of the European luxury industry, as analyzed in the previous chapter. Its sales rose from €102 million in 1992 to 296 million in 2000 and almost 1.9 billion in the 2015–16 financial year (Chart 3.2). This success resulted from a new strategy implemented in the second half of the 1990s, which fundamentally changed the nature of the company. Before this transformation, CDC was a small company with high profitability: 132 million in 1992–5, and its profit rate (operating profit) was over 15 percent of sales. Within twenty years, it had become a large company with high profitability. The profit rate since 2012 has been over 10 percent, but the total value of profits is twenty times higher than in the early 1990s. CDC is now a cash machine and a financial success story. However, this success has taken time and substantial investment. The years 1997–2001 were a period of transition and low profitability (average profit rate of 2.5 percent) before the company returned to a continuous growth dynamic—except during the global financial crisis of 2008–10.

The Dior brand heritage strategy is at the heart of CDC's tremendous expansion into global markets. Before discussing the process of building and managing this heritage, it is necessary to understand the context in which the transformation took shape. Three main elements underpin this transformation: investment in the sales network, the strengthening of control over diversification through accessories, and the engagement of star designers.

First, until the early 1990s, sales of Dior clothing and accessories were made through independent retailers, notably department stores. A few large Dior shops, such as those on Avenue Montaigne in Paris and the one in New York, were owned by CDC, but they were exceptions. In 1992, retail sales represented only 28.2 percent of turnover. The following year, Bernard Arnault, the company's chairman, stated that the company's growth required "the creation of a network of boutiques."[17] Therefore, during the 1990s, CDC opened sales subsidiaries around the world to implement direct sales of its products. Contracts with local retailers were broken—for example, in Malaysia (1994), Monaco (1994), Hong Kong (1995), Singapore (1996), Japan (1997), Taiwan (1997), and South Korea (1997). Then, dozens of Dior mono-brand boutiques opened around the world. DCC had 73 such stores in 1999 when it first published this information. Chart 3.3 shows the impact of this new distribution strategy. The share of retail sales in the turnover exceeded the 50 percent mark in 1997 and reached 71.7 percent in 2000. The number of shops also continued to grow strongly until the global financial crisis, peaking at 237 in 2008 and 2009 before declining slightly owing to the closure of unprofitable

Figure 3.3 Dior flagship store, New York, 2019.
Source: Wikimedia Commons
https://commons.wikimedia.org/wiki/File:Dior_NYC_Flagship_(48064046348).jpg?uselang=fr

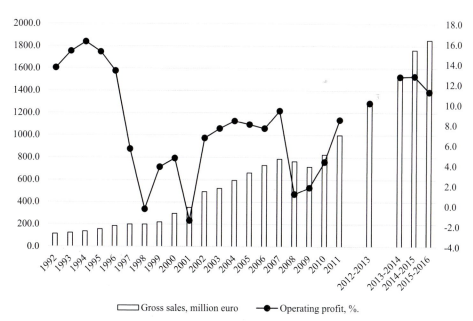

Chart 3.2 Christian Dior Couture SA, turnover in € million and profit rate in %, 1992–2016.
Source: Christian Dior Couture SA, *Annual Reports.*
Note: Fiscal years are calendar years until 2011, then May–April in 2012–13 and July–June since 2013–14. The periods January–April 2011 and May–June 2013 are not included in this chart.

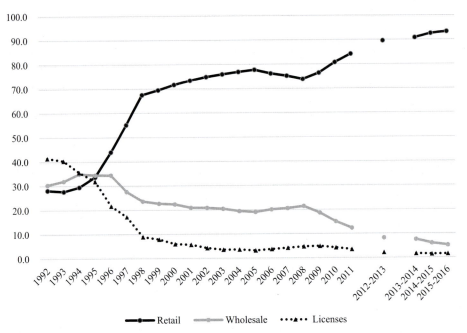

Chart 3.3 Composition of CDC turnover, in %, 1992–2016.
Source: See Chart 3.2.

shops (200 shops in 2016). The average value of sales per shop, which varied between €2.2 and 2.7 million in 2000–8, rose to 4 million in 2011 and 8.8 million in 2015–16. Sales, therefore, generated a growing amount of money and their importance in CDC's turnover has continued to grow since 2000, even exceeding 90 percent since the 2013–14 fiscal year.

Mono-brand boutiques play a major role in the global expansion of European luxury brands.[18] In its 1994 annual report, CDC describes their role as follows:

> The development [of the network] is mainly a response to the desire to offer Christian Dior's customers luxurious boutiques that reinforce the prestige of the brand; to broaden the distribution of exclusive products, particularly in the women's ready-to-wear or accessories sector, marketed only in the brand boutiques.[19]

The boutiques are not only points of sale but also help transmit the brand's values to consumers. They are in themselves integrated into the storytelling strategy of the brands, as we will see below.

The second characteristic of CDC's transformation was the strong centralization of control over product diversification. From the 1950s to the early 1990s, Christian Dior's international expansion was based largely on licensing agreements and the local production of a multiplicity of Dior-branded accessories.[20] However, such a practice posed problems for image control and building a strong brand for the global market.

Also, at the beginning of the 1990s, Bernard Arnault announced his intention to take charge of "the development of direct activities"[21]—that is, the diversification of products. The aim was not to eliminate the production and sale of accessories, which represented an essential source of profit and made it possible to broaden the brand's customer base. The launch of the Lady Dior handbag in 1995, which was a great success worldwide, shows the considerable financial impact of a successful diversification strategy for accessories. The challenge was to regain control over the products distributed under the Dior label worldwide and integrate them into a global strategy—in line with the brand's heritage. CDC thus broke the licensing agreements for ladies' ready-to-wear in Europe (1994), menswear and leather goods in the United States (1995), ready-to-wear and accessories in Japan (1998), and lingerie and pantyhose for the whole world (2002). As a result, the share of licenses in turnover fell sharply from 41.1 percent in 1992 to 5.1 percent in 2000.

Since 2000, CDC has gradually taken control of "strategic licences"[22] for fashion accessories sold in boutiques. It took a minority stake in the Italian sunglasses manufacturer Safilo (2001), acquired a German jewelry manufacturer (2005) and acquired 87 percent of the capital of John Galliano SA, a company involved in the design of various luxury and fashion items (2008). The integration into the LVMH group also allowed the company to benefit from the expertise of John Galliano SA—for example, in the manufacture of watches. The acquisition of several Swiss watch brands at the end of the 1990s led to an internalization of the capacity to design and manufacture watches,

Figure 3.4 Dior perfume, Osaka, 2016.
Source: author.

which was put at the service of the group's various fashion brands, from Dior to Vuitton. In 2001, LVMH founded Ateliers Horlogers SA in Switzerland, which is responsible for this function.[23] The production of all accessories was not internalized but strictly controlled by the Paris headquarters. In 1996, CDC explained that the:

> ... closer collaboration [with licensees] has made it possible to improve the coherence of the style, and to decline certain emblematic Christian Dior themes for accessories with great success (such as the use of the "cannage" theme on the sunglasses, for example).[24]

Finally, the third characteristic of Dior's transformation was the hiring of a new generation of star designers. In 1994, Arnault stressed the need to "strengthen and renew the creative teams."[25] The Italian couturier Gianfranco Ferré, Dior's artistic director since 1989, created classic haute couture and ready-to-wear in the tradition of Christian Dior himself and his successor Marc Bohan. This positioning, however, made it hard to create a strong fashion brand for the global luxury market. Thus, in 1996, Arnault appointed a new artistic director in the person of the British designer John Galliano, to whom he had already entrusted the management of Givenchy, another LVMH brand, a year earlier. Galliano's eccentric personality and the provocative and iconoclastic nature of his shows and communication—he was one of the promoters of porno chic in France—contributed to a profound transformation of Dior's image, which became an expression of contemporary fashion and glamour.[26] In 2000, Arnault explained:

> John Galliano has unquestionably brought a new vision of fashion and his style has set a standard. Commercial success was not long in coming and sales of women's ready-to-wear have risen sharply since his arrival.[27]

John Galliano himself told French journalists in the same year that his shows aimed to bring "extreme ideas"[28] into fashion, which were not yet present in the brand's shops. This promise had a great media impact. Despite his undeniable success, Galliano was fired from Dior in 2011 following a scandal involving racist and anti-Semitic slurs in a Parisian public house.[29] The fashion genius had become damaging to the Dior brand and was replaced by Belgian designer Raf Simons (2012) and then by Maria Grazia Chiuri (2016), an Italian fashion designer who specialized in the development of accessories and had previously worked for Fendi and Valentino.

In addition, along with Galliano, CDC hired two other designers who contributed to the transformation of Dior. In 1998, Victoire de Castellane, who had spent her entire career at Chanel, became the first artistic director of Dior Joaillerie. She took charge of the development of jewelry at Dior when licenses were ending, and the Paris headquarters was resuming control over the production of accessories. A Dior jewelry boutique was opened under her management at Place Vendôme in 2001. A year earlier, in 2000, CDC had entrusted men's fashion to the avant-garde designer Hedi Slimane. He was replaced in 2007 by his assistant Kris Van Assche, a Belgian designer who had previously worked for Yves

Saint Laurent. Since Galliano, CDC has hired several designers from a small community of avant-garde designers working in the leading French and Italian fashion houses. They did not maintain the "real" Christian Dior style but developed creative activities that helped reinforce Dior's image as one of the promoters of fashion as artistic expression. The role of the designers was once again emphasized by Bernard Arnault in 2001:

> Thanks to its creative and very high quality products that meet the expectations of a young and refined clientele, Christian Dior has achieved a formidable commercial breakthrough. It is, without question, the greatest success story in the world of fashion today.[30]

3.3 Building the Dior heritage

Dior's tremendous expansion since the 1990s flowed from a profound transformation of the company, marked by growing centralization and control by the Paris headquarters over creation, diversification into accessories, and the distribution system. This break with the past allowed for the creation of a strong brand for the global market. What role did tradition play in this process? How have Dior's managers used the company's past to implement a heritage strategy that places the brand in a coherent and appealing narrative?

First, Bernard Arnault and the management of CDC constantly insist on the continuity of the Dior brand throughout time and the permanence of its heritage. Since the 1990s, the main values of the brand have been glamorous elegance, modern style, and the revolutionary character of its artistic creation. These values are communicated to the general public through advertising campaigns in the Dior boutiques, as well as through the organization of major events such as the centenary in 2005 of Christian Dior's birth, or the sixtieth (2007) and seventieth (2017) anniversaries of the company's foundation. These events are often hosted by prestigious museums that give legitimacy to the storytelling proposed by the brand.[31] A Christian Dior museum was opened in the designer's house in the North of France in the 1990s. In 2006, Arnault stated:

> ... the values of elegance and innovation, which have carried the House since its creation in 1947, are echoing ever more powerfully in a world in search of creativity and extreme quality. In keeping with Christian Dior's ambition to export his fashion to the five continents, the House is now reaching out to new customers to offer them exceptional products in a prestigious and refined setting.[32]

This discourse on the continuity of a tradition of artistic creation in the field of fashion is, however, only partially consistent with historical reality. The latter is tinkered with to make the construction of a coherent legacy possible. This is why Dior is ideal for analyzing the process of building heritage.

It should be remembered that Christian Dior himself was not a couturier who wanted to revolutionize artistic creation in the field of fashion. His shows were not intended to shock the public or create media impact for the brand but appeal to his upper-middle-class clientele. He was a classic and conservative, even reactionary, couturier. According to the feminist journalist Françoise Giroud, Dior was:

> frightened of change, which he abhorred; he loved closed gardens, closed beds, maternal women, everything that made him feel protected. Absolutely French in his refinement and his taste for moderation, he hated exoticism, at least in fashion.[33]

He thus has nothing to do with Galliano's fanciful dimension.

Born in 1905, Christian Dior worked in the Parisian haute couture houses of Piguet and Lelong before launching his own company after the Second World War, thanks to the capital of textile magnate Marcel Boussac.[34] He became world-famous with the launch of his first collection in 1947, described by an American journalist as the "New Look." After the austerity of the war years, Dior proposed a style of full skirts, tight waists and jackets with rounded shoulders that emphasized the woman's body—and drew criticism from the avant-gardists, such as Coco Chanel, who had been working on the emancipation of women in fashion during the interwar years.[35] Christian Dior was, therefore, not a revolutionary couturier. He produced fashion that corresponded to the expectations of his bourgeois clientele. Christian Dior SA was a profitable company that expanded greatly in Europe, the United States, Latin America, and Japan. The business model of the company, the largest employer in the Paris fashion industry in the early 1950s, focused on creating haute couture in Paris and signing licenses to enter foreign markets.

After the sudden death of Christian Dior in 1957, his assistant, Yves Saint Laurent, took over the artistic direction of the company. His position was at odds with that of his mentor. He was a modernist who wanted to explore new forms of fashion, but his radical approach did not suit Dior's traditional clientele.[36] Saint Laurent left Christian Dior SA in 1960 and opened his own house. He was replaced by a classic couturier, Marc Bohan, who had begun his career at Patou. As artistic director until 1989, Bohan continued and developed the model established by Christian Dior, namely the concentration of activities on Parisian haute couture and ready-to-wear, as well as the strengthening of international growth through the development of licenses around the world. The latter became the primary source of profit.[37] In 1968, the Boussac group, owner of Christian Dior SA, turned the perfume division into an autonomous company, Parfums Christian Dior SA, and sold 50% of the capital to the champagne house Moët & Chandon (which increased its participation to 70 percent in 1971). Boussac needed new money to bail out the deficit of its textile activities, but it was unable to escape bankruptcy. The group was taken over in 1984 by businessman Bernard Arnault, whose aim was to get his hands on Christian Dior SA and the department store Le Bon Marché, which also belonged to Boussac. Arnault was obviously inspired by the success of Chanel after the arrival of Karl Lagerfeld at its head in 1983.[38]

In 1989, Arnault appointed a new artistic director to whom he entrusted not only haute couture and ready-to-wear, as Bohan had done, but the entire brand identity. Italian designer Gianfranco Ferré, who held the position from 1989 to 1996, dusted off the image of the Dior brand with his glamorous fashion shows for the presentation of haute couture creations, as well as the launch of iconic accessories such as the Lady Dior

Figure 3.5 Exhibition Christian Dior in Moscow, 2011.
Source: Wikimedia Commons.
https://commons.wikimedia.org/wiki/File:Christian_Dior_(Moscow_exhibition,_2011)_10.jpg

bag. He was assisted by a director of the accessories division, a position newly created in 1992 and held by a financial professional.[39] However, the company, listed on the stock exchange in 1991, experienced only weak growth (Chart 3.2). The necessary breakthrough came with the hiring of Galliano in 1996.

The arrival of Galliano corresponded to the adoption of a new discourse that resulted from the construction of heritage. Dior became the embodiment of artistic creation in fashion from the mid-twentieth century and continued this positioning throughout the world. Christian Dior himself was portrayed as a revolutionary couturier. In 2020, the company's website page dedicated to its history opened with the following words:

Christian Dior changed the codes of global elegance with his first collection in 1947. This vision is passed on today with boldness and inventiveness.[40]

Figure 3.6 Christian Dior with six of his models after a fashion parade at the Savoy Hotel, London, 1950.
Source: Getty Image, ID: 3352130
Credit: Fred Ramage / Stringer

The brand's storytelling made the founding elements of Dior (the Bar suit and the New Look style) the basis for everything the company has done ever since:

> More than six decades after its birth, the New Look revolution and its spirit continue to inspire Dior. The New Look is a perpetual revolution.[41]

This legacy of revolutionary artistic creation was a simple and powerful message that helped make Dior an extremely well-positioned and appealing global brand. Although Galliano's work was essentially a deconstruction of Christian Dior's classic work, Galliano presented himself early in his career as an heir to Dior, presenting modernized versions of the Bar suit, a practice continued by his successors. Moreover, in 1985, CDC decided to set up a historical archive department, which included drawings and creations made since 1947. Later renamed Dior Heritage, this department allowed the brand's artistic directors since Galliano to draw, from Dior's past, various elements and graphic references used in contemporary creations.[42] In another sign of the New Look in current communication, the exhibition, organized in Paris for the company's seventieth anniversary in 2017, opened by presenting the Bar suit in the main hall before visitors followed the evolution of the creations in the various rooms of the Musée des Arts Décoratifs.

Finally, the Dior boutiques themselves became embodiments of the brand's heritage. Whereas the old outlets from the 1950s to the 1970s sought to replicate the classic Louis XVI-style atmosphere of the Parisian shop, the new mono-brand shops opened after 1990 were works of contemporary art.[43] American architect Peter Marino, a celebrity in modern art and luxury circles, was commissioned to renovate the interior design of the Dior shops in the mid-1990s.

3.4 Conclusion

The example of Christian Dior, presented in detail in this chapter, shows that the international expansion and transformation into the big business of the European luxury industry during the 1980s and 1990s was based on the exploitation of a new resource: brand heritage. Through identity bricolage, heritage allowed strong coherence between the goods and the narratives developed by the brands. A catchy message, embodied by the products, sometimes conveyed by renowned ambassadors, and aimed at a clearly identified clientele, made it possible to build a strong brand on the global market. This is all the more essential now. Since the 1990s, the growth of luxury companies has depended on the democratization of consumption. The transition from an upper-middle-class clientele, intimate with the manufacturers of luxury products, to mass consumption, implies the need for brands that convey simple, coherent messages.

Figure 3.7 Dior store, Charles de Gaulle airport, Paris, 2019.
Source: author.

PART II
THE ACTORS OF THE GLOBAL LUXURY INDUSTRY

The transformation process of the luxury industry presented in Part I is a general model implemented in different ways by the companies. Part II now presents the different organizational models of the global luxury industry. It opens with an analysis of the formation and development of conglomerates, in particular LVMH. These conglomerates represent the dominant type of firm in this industry; however, other types of firms coexist within these conglomerates. They have specificities in terms of governance, product specialization and presence outside of luxury itself, factors discussed below. A total of five organizational models of luxury companies are identified: conglomerates, independent family businesses, industrial groups, brands with deep regional roots, and new luxury players.

CHAPTER 4
A DOMINANT PLAYER—THE DIVERSIFIED CONGLOMERATES

The diversified conglomerates, LVMH, Richemont and Kering, now dominate the global luxury goods industry. In 2017, they were, respectively, the largest, third-largest, and fourth-largest company in the sector, with combined sales of almost $53 billion, or 21.5 percent of the sales of the top 100 luxury companies. The second-largest is the US cosmetics manufacturer The Estée Lauder Company (Table 2.1).

These companies are of considerable importance not only because of their size but also because of the business model they adopted during the 1990s. They have profoundly transformed the luxury industry. Their strategy, organization and management practices have become models for smaller, more specialized companies, whether they are involved in fashion, cosmetics, watches, or jewelry. However, the process of creating these groups during the 1980s and 1990s and their growth remains relatively unknown. Only a few works have analyzed these phenomena in broad terms.[1] Furthermore, we must ask ourselves what the competitive advantage of these diversified conglomerates is.

4.1 Moët Hennessy–Louis Vuitton (LVMH)

The French group Moët Hennessy–Louis Vuitton (LVMH), today the undisputed leader in the global luxury goods industry, resulted from the 1987 merger of two small family-owned companies that needed new money to continue their growth and expansion around the world.[2] The first was the travel goods and leather goods manufacturer Louis Vuitton, a small company that experienced tremendous growth in the early 1980s. The company's sales rose from €51.7 million in 1981 to 213.4 million in 1985, thanks to the Asian markets (17 percent of the total in 1981 and 44 percent in 1985).[3] In 1986, the profits were reinvested in the purchase of Veuve Clicquot, which owned several champagne brands and the company Parfums Givenchy. The second company, Moët Hennessy, was founded in 1971 when champagne (Moët & Chandon) and cognac (Hennessy) producers merged. Moët & Chandon had previously acquired other champagne manufacturers (Ruinart in 1962, Mercier in 1970) and had diversified into cosmetics with the purchase of RoC and Parfums Christian Dior (1971).

The 1987 merger was, therefore, part of a consolidation of the luxury perfume and champagne sectors. It was made possible by the financial support of two French banks (Lazard Frères and Paribas), but the owners of the two merged companies retained control of LVMH thanks to preference shares that gave them special voting rights (55 percent of the votes for 37 percent of the capital). With the financial support of the

Figure 4.1 The construction of a French world leader: LVMH, conference at École Polytechnique, Paris, 2017.

Source: Wikimedia Commons.
https://commons.wikimedia.org/wiki/File:Conf%C3%A9rence_%C3%A0_l%27Ecole_polytechnique_de_
Bernard_Arnault_%22LVMH,_la_construction_d%27un_leader_mondial_Fran%C3%A7ais%22_
(33413492076).jpg?uselang=fr

British group Guinness, Bernard Arnault, a minority shareholder in LVMH, managed to buy out the shares of Henri Racamier, the director of Louis Vuitton, who was in conflict with his partner in Moët Hennessy. Thus, Arnault took control of LVMH.[4] A few years earlier, he had already acquired the textile group Boussac (1984–5), which itself owned the haute couture house Christian Dior. In 1987, Arnault also bought the leather goods manufacturer Céline and invested in the fashion house Christian Lacroix.[5] He aimed to bring together various French luxury brands within a single group. LVMH was originally a purely French business, combining fashion, champagne, cognac, and perfume. In 1991, 66.8 percent of the group's employees were active in France.

Chart 4.1 shows the organization of LVMH at the time of the takeover by Bernard Arnault. The takeover had two characteristics. Firstly, the new owner's strategy of purchase and control was typical of a form of Mediterranean capitalism observed elsewhere in France and Italy in the second half of the twentieth century.[6] Rather than relying heavily on the financial markets, as would be the case in the United States, a pyramidal organizational structure was set up, with numerous intermediaries (Arnault & Associés, Financière Agache, Jacques Rober). This structure allowed a single entrepreneur to control companies without directly owning the majority of their capital. The challenge was to find partners at each level willing to invest minority shares, but some French banks and Guinness were attracted by Arnault's project and supported it. Secondly, despite the creation of a new company (LVMH), the organization of the group remained decentralized. Louis Vuitton and Moët-Hennessy continued to control their own subsidiaries, with the exception of Parfums Dior. There was no rationalization in terms of product families.

In the mid-1990s, LVMH restructured its internal organization, grouping its various subsidiaries into product families. Louis Vuitton oversaw the fashion brands, while Moët Hennessy managed the spirits brands. In addition, in 1994, LVMH signed a new agreement with Guinness (merged into Diageo in 1997), whereby Guinness received 34 percent of Moët Hennessy and continued its cooperation with LVMH for the worldwide distribution of alcoholic beverages. The Irish brewer also withdrew from LVMH, while LVMH reduced its stake in Guinness from 24 percent to 20 percent. This operation produced €3 billion in cash, which was used to buy new luxury companies. Many of these were non-French, and their acquisition marks the first phase of LVMH's internationalization. In fashion, for example, it purchased the Japanese designer Kenzo (1993), the French shoe manufacturer Berluti (1996), the Spanish brand Loewe (1996), and acquired a majority stake in the company of New York designer Marc Jacobs (1997). In perfumery, LVMH took over Guerlain (1994). Finally, the French group strengthened its position in retail by taking a majority stake in the Hong Kong company DFS, which ran duty-free shops around the world (1996), and by acquiring Sephora, the largest French perfume and cosmetics chain (1997).

As a result of this expansion, the conglomerate's balance sheet quadrupled during the 1990s, from €4.8 billion in 1989 to 20.7 billion in 1999 (Chart 4.2, page 65). However, this tremendous expansion was not based solely on the cash from the new Guinness deal, but also on debt. Their equity share declined during this decade, dropping to a low of 28.9 percent of assets in 2001. Moreover, although gross sales grew from €3 billion in 1990 to 11.6 billion in 2000, gross profit declined from 28.6 percent to 16.9 percent over the same period.

LVMH needed a new strategy to ensure continued growth in the early twenty-first century, especially as the Chinese market offered exciting prospects. Arnault decided to focus on luxury goods and establish himself as the world leader in this industry. He divested several businesses that did not fit this positioning, such as the US cosmetics companies Hard Candy and Urban Decay (2002) and the Swiss watch company Ebel (2004). He also sold minority shares in the auction house Phillips, de Pury & Luxembourg (2003) and the company of American designer Michael Kors (2003). Finally, in 2003, LVMH divested itself of the cognac manufacturer Hine and the champagne producer Canard-Duchêne to strengthen its other brands active in these sectors.

At the same time, LVMH continued to expand with the acquisition of luxury companies in various countries. It took over the fashion designers Thomas Pink in Britain (1999), Emilio Pucci in Italy (2000), and Donna Karan in the United States (2001; sold in 2016). From 2001, it also tried to take control of Hermès, an independent company listed on the Paris Stock Exchange, by buying back shares through a system of shell companies. In 2013, LVMH held 22 percent of its competitor, a situation that led to

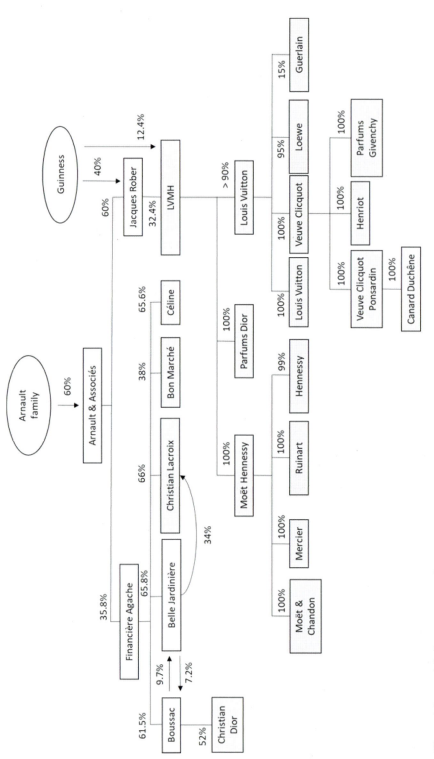

Chart 4.1 Simplified organization of LVMH, 1987.

Source: Made by the author based on Eurostaf Dafsa, *LVMH*, 1987.

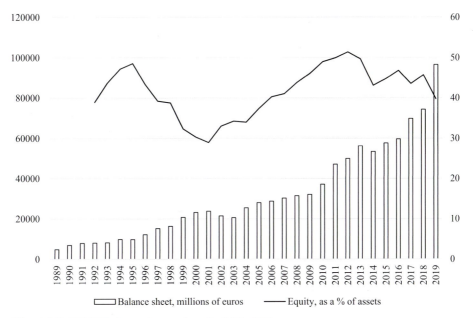

Chart 4.2 LVMH balance sheet and equity, 1989–2019.
Source: LVMH, annual reports and reference documents, 1989–2019.
Note: The increase in the balance sheet in 2019 is largely due to a change in French law recognizing the rights of use of boutiques leased by LVMH (rental value). They represent a capital gain of €12.4 billion.

violent conflict between the two companies.[7] An agreement was reached in the following years, and LVMH disposed of its Hermès shares. The conglomerate used the cash from this transaction to buy out minority shareholders in Christian Dior Couture and integrate the latter into LVMH (2017).[8] In addition, LVMH entered the watch industry in 1999 with the acquisition of the Swiss watch manufacturers Tag Heuer and Zenith, followed by Hublot in 2008. Already present in the jewelry market with the acquisition of Fred in 1995, LVMH strengthened its foothold in this field with the takeover of another French jeweler, Chaumet (1999), the creation of a joint venture with the South African company De Beers, which controlled the world diamond market (2001; liquidated in 2017), as well as the takeovers of the Italian company Bulgari (2011) and the American company Tiffany (2020). It also diversified its portfolio of alcohol brands with the acquisitions of Krug champagne (1999), the famous Château d'Yquem vineyard (1999), the prestige vodka maker Millennium (2004), Glenmorangie whisky (2005), and the Chinese distillery Wen Jun (2007). Finally, in 2018, LVMH diversified into luxury travel with the acquisition of Belmond. In 2019, LVMH comprised a total of seventy brands.

All these investments transformed LVMH into a giant in the global luxury industry. The number of employees grew from about 14,000 in 1990 to over 47,000 in 2000 and over 156,000 in 2019. In that year, the proportion of staff employed in France was 20 percent. This expansion was based on the acquisition of companies, which enabled very strong growth, as shown by the increase in the balance sheet. Its value rose from €23.2 billion in 2000 to 95.7 billion in 2019, a development made possible without increasing the debt. The share of equity even rose sharply until 2012 (51.4 percent) before entering a period of decline. As for Bernard Arnault, he permanently retained control over the group thanks to the majority of votes conferred on him by his preference shares (47.2 percent of the capital and 63.4 percent of the votes in 2018). LVMH's independence is due to its high profitability. After a sharp decline in the 1990s owing to numerous investments and the in-depth reorganization of the group, operating profit entered a phase of increase in 2001. Since 2007, it has stabilized at around 20 percent of turnover, in the context of a formidable growth in sales (Chart 4.3). LVMH has become a real cash machine.

The acquisition of dozens of companies around the world presented a great challenge in financial and organizational terms, and it made LVMH in 2019 a very different company from what it had been thirty years earlier. Vertical integration and product divisions had, over the years, improved the management of brand portfolios that were active in the same market. Coordination within a product family started with champagne (1995) and perfumery (1997) before being extended to the whole group. In 1998, the divisional organization was completed (Chart 4.4). It was perfected in 2017 when LVMH bought Christian Dior Couture and integrated it into its fashion division. Despite this new structure at the level of the operating companies, LVMH retained its pyramidal organization at the level of the shareholder base.

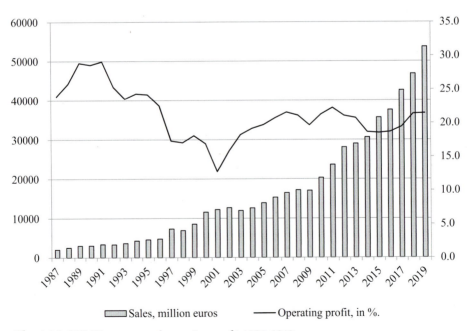

Chart 4.3 LVMH revenue and operating profit, 1987–2019.
Source: LVMH, annual reports and reference documents, 1989–2019.

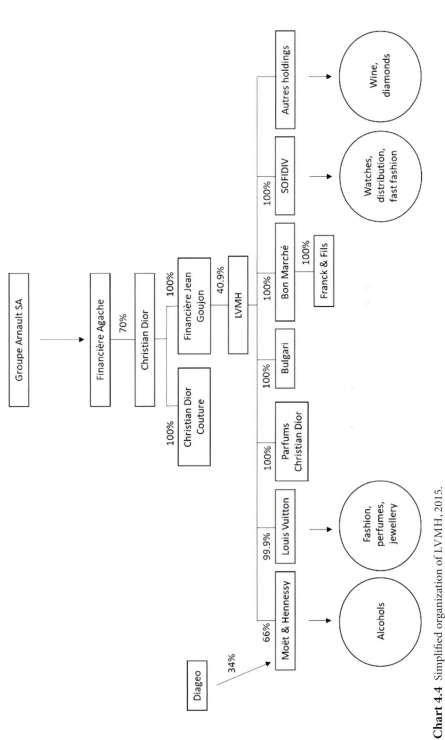

Chart 4.4 Simplified organization of LVMH, 2015.
Source: Made by the author based on LVMH, reference document, 2015.

4.2 Compagnie Financière Richemont

The birth of Compagnie Financière Richemont in 1988 resulted from an encounter between French entrepreneurs who had taken over the jeweler Cartier and a South African investor, Anton Rupert. Since its foundation in mid-nineteenth century Paris, Cartier had been a small family business specializing in the production and sale of jewelry for the aristocracy and upper-middle class. Its business model did not change fundamentally for more than a century, but Cartier faced financial difficulties and declining profitability in the 1960s. In 1972, French businessman Robert Hocq, an industrialist producing Cartier lighters under license since 1968, and financier Joseph Kanoui took over the jeweler. Under the direction of Alain-Dominique Perrin, the company launched the "Must de Cartier" concept in 1973. It repositioned the brand in the accessible luxury segment and focused on producing accessories such as lighters and watches. In the following years, Kanoui bought Cartier sales companies in the United

Figure 4.2 The Richemont group was born out of the takeover of Cartier and its transformation into an accessible luxury brand for the global market. Here, a Cartier flagship store under construction at the Wuhan International Plaza Shopping Centre, China, 2009.
Source: Getty Image, ID: 84960920
Credit: China Photos / Stringer

States and Great Britain. He also opened a factory in Switzerland for the production of accessories in 1979.[9] However, the company's development required fresh capital. The new owners turned to Anton Rupert, an entrepreneur and investor from South Africa who wanted to diversify his assets. He bought Cartier in 1988.

The Rupert family had made their fortune in mining, tobacco, finance, media, and luxury goods. In 1988, the seventy-year-old patriarch, Anton Rupert, decided to found Richemont to manage all his foreign investments. He established the firm in the Swiss tax haven of Zug. Joseph Kanoui was a member of the board of directors.[10] Richemont is listed on the Zurich Stock Exchange, but the Rupert family members retain control through the ownership of preference shares, which give them preferential voting rights. In 2019, the financial company controlled by the family (Compagnie Financière Rupert) held 9.1 percent of Richemont's capital but 50 percent of the voting rights.

At its foundation, Richemont had five divisions arranged according to their field of activity: luxury, tobacco, finance, natural resources (mining), and consumer goods. The luxury division included two companies (Cartier and Dunhill), which in turn controlled other luxury brands, including a license for the production and sale of Yves Saint Laurent and Ferrari accessories (held by Cartier), and the Montblanc and Chloé brands (held by Dunhill). In the same year, Cartier acquired two Swiss watch companies, Piaget and Baume & Mercier. In 1993, the group's various luxury companies merged into a new entity, the Vendôme Group, as a division of Richemont.[11] This group acquired and integrated new luxury companies in several countries: the British firearms manufacturer Purdey (1994), the watch companies Vacheron & Constantin in Switzerland (1996), and Officine Panerai in Italy (1996), as well as the French leather goods company Lancel (1996) and the Hong Kong fashion brand Shanghai Tang (1998). Most of these were small, independent, mostly family-owned businesses that needed fresh capital to continue their expansion. As a result, Richemont's balance sheet increased from £2.9 billion in 1990 ($5.2 billion) to £5 billion in 1998 ($8.3 billion), with a high share of equity that showed a general trend of stability during this period (average of 66 percent) (Chart 4.5).

However, Richemont was still a diversified conglomerate, heavily involved in tobacco and television until the late 1990s. In 1997, the Vendôme luxury division represented only 31.3 percent of turnover and 25.5 percent of profits. A strategic change took place between 1999 and 2005, characterized by an increasing concentration on luxury. Firstly, Richemont divested its interest in the television group Canal+ (2000). It also sold the British clothing company Hackett (2005). Finally, it gradually reduced its involvement in tobacco—this division being transferred in 2008 to Reinet Investments, a financial company also controlled by the Rupert family. The company's profitability, which fell sharply in 1999–2003, rose again until 2015 (Chart 4.6). Thus, Richemont gradually established itself as a group specializing in luxury goods. It transferred its headquarters from the canton of Zug to the city of Geneva, a city closer to Paris and a breeding ground for talented managers specializing in luxury.[12]

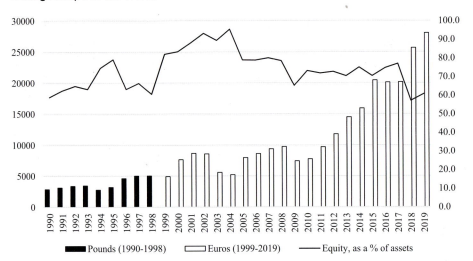

Chart 4.5 Richemont's balance sheet, in millions of pounds and euros, and equity share, in %, 1990–2019.

Source: Compagnie Financière Richemont, *Annual Reports*, 1990–2019.

Note: Fiscal years end in March (2019: April 2018 to March 2019).

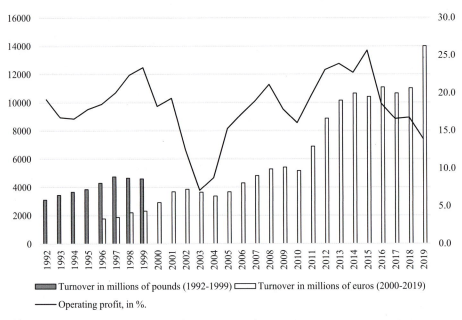

Chart 4.6 Richemont's turnover and operating results, 1992–2019.

Source: Compagnie Financière Richemont, *Annual Reports*, 1992–2019.

Note: This data also includes the non-luxury divisions for turnover in pounds, but only the luxury division for turnover in euros.

Since the 2008 reorganization, Richemont's structure has been relatively simple. It is a holding company comprising four divisions in which the various brands are grouped according to their activity (jewelry; watches; online distribution; fashion and accessories). The holding company ensures coordination between the brands and offers a series of centralized services (finance, legal affairs, logistics, production, marketing, etc.) as well as regional services throughout the world (after-sales service, human resources, real estate, etc.). By freeing up cash, this reorganization has enabled the group to purchase companies without needing to open up the capital or resort too much to bank credit, thus strengthening its presence in the luxury goods sector. Initially, the divestments led to a reduction in the balance sheet (€7.6 billion in 2000 and €5.2 billion in 2004) and an increase in the share of equity, which reached a peak of 95.5 percent in 2004. This financial independence made it possible to buy up many companies while retaining control of the group. Indeed, the balance sheet has grown enormously to date (more than €28 billion in 2019), and autonomy remains high despite the downward trend in the share of equity, which remained at 60.8 percent in 2019 (Chart 4.5 above). Richemont's strong development since 2005 has also been due to wide profit margins, with profits rising from 7.1 percent in 2003 to a peak of more than 25 percent in 2015, before undergoing a phase of decline because of the difficulties encountered by the luxury watch industry in Hong Kong and China.

The expansion of the group took the form of acquiring several companies during the reorganization phase, including the French jeweler Van Cleef & Arpels (1999), the Swiss watchmakers Jaeger-LeCoultre (2000), and IWC Schaffhausen (2000), and the German watch manufacturer A. Lange & Söhne (2000). Since the mid-2000s, Richemont has been buying up several watch-component manufacturers to gain better control over its supply— it largely depended on the Swatch Group for the acquisition of movements and parts—and has been investing in the development of its production capabilities, with the takeover of Minerva (2006), a watch factory that began by designing watches for Montblanc. It also took over the watch-case manufacturer Donzé-Baume SA (2007). Richemont also signed a licensing agreement with Ralph Lauren for the manufacture and sale of watches under the American designer's brand (2008) and acquired the small watch manufacturer Roger Dubuis in Geneva (2008). The fashion division was strengthened by the purchase of the Parisian house Azzedine Alaïa (2007) and the American brand Peter Millar (2012). Finally, Richemont took a majority stake in Net-A-Porter Group, one of the leading online luxury fashion retailers (2010). Five years later, this company merged with the Italian company Yoox, which operates in the same market. Finally, in 2018, Richemont created a joint venture with Chinese web giant Alibaba, which specializes in the online sale of fashion products in China including major global brands not owned by the Swiss conglomerate.[13]

Control of a global distribution network and the ability to invest heavily in retail are two major competitive advantages of conglomerates. Richemont's commitment to online sales is part of a growing verticalization of sales activities in group-owned shops rather than through wholesalers. The share of wholesalers fell from 70.5 percent in 1995 to 31.2 percent in 2019. Richemont now has direct control over most of its sales, both in shops (52.4 percent in 2019) and online (16.4 percent).

Figure 4.3 François Pinault (R), his son François-Henri Pinault (L), CEO and Chairman of Kering, his grandson François Pinault and Paris Mayor Anne Hidalgo (C) pose after a press conference to announce the project to install the art collection of François Pinault at the Paris Commercial Exchange, Paris, 2016.
Source: Getty Image, ID: 524930826
Credit: Chesnot / Contributor.

4.3 Kering

The third-largest luxury conglomerate, Kering, is a French company that specialized in retail. In 1999, it repositioned itself in luxury goods with a stake in the Italian fashion company Gucci. Kering's origins date back to the founding of an international timber and building materials trading company by François Pinault in 1963.[14] Pinault SA remained focused on these areas of activity during the 1970s and 1980s. In 1988, it was listed on the Paris Stock Exchange in order to increase its capital and diversify in other retail sectors. It acquired Compagnie Française d'Afrique Occidentale (CFAO), a company selling electrical equipment and importing and exporting to Africa (1990), the furniture chain store Conforama (1991) and Au Printemps group, which includes the eponymous Parisian department store, the Prisunic convenience store chain and the mail-order house La Redoute (1992). In 1994, after this last acquisition, the group was renamed Pinault-Printemps-Redoute (PPR) and became one of the largest retail companies in France.

However, despite the opening of its capital to new investors, the Pinault family maintains control over the company through the ownership of special shares that grant preferential voting rights. In 1987, before the IPO, François Pinault created a new company, Financière Pinault, which, according to the French media, is entirely controlled

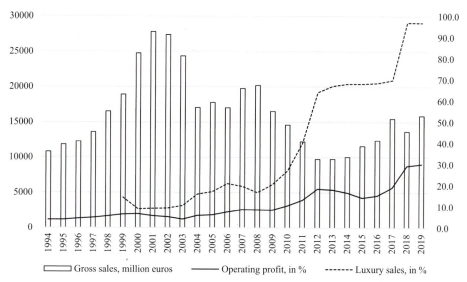

Chart 4.7 PPR–Kering sales and operating income, 1994–2019.
Source: PPR–Kering, *Annual Report*, 1994–2019.

by his family.[15] Financière Pinault holds the entire capital of another financial company, Artemis SA, founded in 1992 to manage the various investments of the Pinault family.[16] Thus, Artemis is the main shareholder of PPR. In 1998, it held 42.7 percent of its capital and 58.2 percent of the voting rights. These proportions remained similar until recently (41 percent and 58.1 percent, respectively, in 2019). Thus, Pinault can attract cash from external investors, who enter the capital of PPR, without losing control of his company.

In the second half of the 1990s, PPR continued its expansion strategy in retailing, notably with the purchase of the Fnac chain of record and book shops (1995). A series of acquisitions and partnerships also enabled it to expand internationally, but dependence on the French (55.8 percent of sales in 1998) and European (21.9 percent) markets remained high. As for profit, it was certainly on an upward trend but remained extremely low, operating income rising from 3.8 percent of turnover in 1994 to 5.5 percent in 1998 (Chart 4.7).

In 1999, PPR made a strategic acquisition that opened the doors to a new industry: luxury. The French retailer acquired 40 percent of Gucci's capital for an estimated value of $2.9 billion.[17] Gucci is a family business founded in Florence in 1923. Specializing in the production and sale of leather goods, it expanded rapidly internationally in the 1960s and 1970s. In 1979, it decided to diversify into the production of accessories by signing licensing agreements with dozens of partners. However, this strategy proved damaging in terms of brand image: Gucci lost its reputation as a luxury company and became perceived as a fashion brand for the general public. The company has faced financial difficulties since the 1980s. In 1988, the Gucci family sold half of the capital (and the remainder in 1993) to a Bahraini investment company, Investcorp. The latter had acquired other luxury brands such as jewelers Tiffany and Chaumet, as well as the Swiss watchmaker Breguet, shortly before. Gucci's new management, led by Tom Ford, a young American designer who joined the company in 1990 and was a promoter of porno chic, was appointed artistic director in 1994. This repositioning was a great success, with sales rising from around $500 million in 1986 to 975 million in 1997.[18] The company was floated on the stock exchange in 1995 and attracted the interest of investors such as PPR and others. In 1999, LVMH acquired 34.4 percent of the Italian designer's capital. PPR then proposed to Gucci to increase its capital and take a 40 percent share, a transaction that also reduced LVMH's share to 20 percent. After a violent court battle, LVMH agreed to sell its shares to PPR in 2001. The animosity and competition between Arnault and Pinault remain, to this day, one of the anecdotal facets of the French luxury industry.

Gucci used the cash provided by PPR in 1999 to build an international luxury group through the acquisition of a portfolio of brands: the French fashion designers Yves Saint Laurent (1999) and Balenciaga (2001), the Italian shoe manufacturer Sergio Rossi (1999), the French jeweler Boucheron (2000), the Swiss watchmaker Bedat & Co. (2000), British designers Alexander McQueen (2000) and Stella McCartney (2001), and Italian leather goods manufacturer Bottega Veneta (2001). These investments had a profound impact on the balance sheet of the PPR group, which rose from €12.6 billion in 1998 to 35 billion in 2001, with a slight decrease in the share of equity (Chart 4.8).

Moreover, the luxury division, although a minority (9.1 percent of PPR's turnover in 2001), was extremely profitable. Operating income amounted to 15.9 percent of sales, compared with 5.6 percent for the group as a whole. Pinault, therefore, decided to reorganize his company and refocus it on luxury goods. This restructuring had three characteristics.

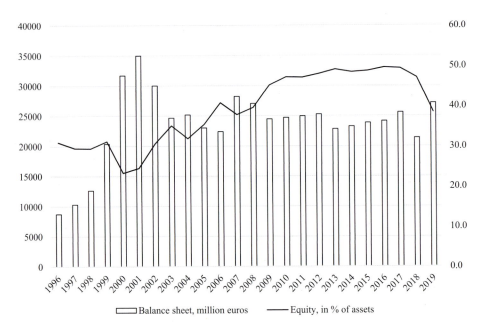

Chart 4.8 PPR–Kering balance sheet and equity, 1996–2019.
Source: PPR–Kering, *Annual Reports*, 1996–2019.

First, PPR withdrew from general retailing by gradually selling off several companies it owned around the world. It abandoned the wood and materials business (2003), sold the Paris department store Le Printemps (2007), and then divested Conforama (2011), Fnac (2013), and La Redoute (2014). Between 2006 and 2011, the share of distribution in the group's turnover fell from 79 percent to 34 percent. These divestments also had a beneficial effect on the balance sheet. In 2009, the balance sheet dipped to €24.5 billion, with equity share rising to 45 percent. In this way, PPR became a smaller, more profitable and more independent company.

Second, the cash generated by these sales, and Gucci's improved profitability, was used to invest in the sports goods business in 2007, with a 27 percent stake in the German company Puma, a proportion that rose to 75 percent in 2011. Considering the tremendous success of Nike and Adidas with their strategy of moving from sports to lifestyle, PPR wanted to do the same with the Puma brand, which had been left behind in this transformation.[19] A lifestyle division was developed through the acquisition of new brands, thanks to the purchase of Dobotex International (2009), Brandon (2009), Cobra (2010), and Volcom (2011). In addition, in 2015, Pinault launched a new subsidiary, Kering Eyewear, specializing in the production of eyewear for the group's various brands, as well as for external customers, notably Cartier (Richemont acquired a stake in Kering Eyewear in 2017). The lifestyle division saw a sharp increase in sales, from €1.7 billion in 2007 to 4.4 billion in 2017, but a significant decrease in profitability: operating income fell from 13.7 percent to 5.7 percent at the same time. As a result, the group divested itself of Puma by selling the majority of its capital to its own shareholders (2017).

Third, the group's luxury division grew based on its developing brands and the reorganization of its portfolio. The expansion of the retail network strongly supported organic growth. The number of directly owned shops was 1,381 in 2019 (including 487 Gucci shops) compared to 196 in 2000 (141 Gucci). Less competitive brands, such as Bedat & Co. (2009), Sergio Rossi (2015), and Stella McCartney (2018), were sold, while PPR acquired Swiss watchmakers Girard Perregaux (23 percent stake in 2008 and 50.1 percent in 2011) and Ulysse Nardin (2014), Chinese jeweler Weelin (2012) and British designer Christopher Kane (2013; sold in 2018). The luxury division showed an impressive development, with sales amounting to €2.5 billion in 2001 and 15.4 billion in 2019, while profitability doubled (15.9 percent in 2001 and 32.8 percent in 2019).

The restructuring of PPR and the refocusing on luxury goods had a considerable impact on the group's finances. Of note, since 2003, the balance sheet has remained remarkably stable at around €25 billion while the share of equity rose continuously until 2017. The group's management is characterized by a desire to strengthen financial independence and profitability through the dynamic management of the brand portfolio. This luxury strategy was implemented by François-Henri Pinault, son of the group's founder, who joined the family group in 1987 and became Chairman and CEO in 2005. The refocusing on luxury is also behind the group's name change to Kering in 2013.

4.4 The competitive advantage of luxury conglomerates

After this presentation of the conditions of formation and development of the three top luxury conglomerates, it is appropriate to discuss the major elements that constitute their strength in the global luxury market. First, let us briefly present the differences between these three groups, which are essentially linked to the extent and diversity of their brand portfolios. A quick look at their balance sheets shows that the size of the conglomerates varies greatly. In 2019, LVMH, the world's largest luxury goods company, had a balance sheet of €96.5 billion, while Richemont had 28 billion and Kering 27.1 billion. LVMH is, therefore, three times larger than its two rivals. Moreover, despite a similar organizational structure, each of the conglomerates offers a particular profile. LVMH is the most diversified, with fashion, champagne and spirits, cosmetics and perfumery, watches and jewelry, retail and hotels. In comparison, Richemont heavily specializes in watches and jewelry (71.9 percent of turnover in 2019), with only a few fashion brands and no cosmetics or spirits brands. As for Kering, it is positioned in luxury fashion, with mainly Gucci (61 percent of turnover in 2019) and Yves Saint Laurent (12 percent). It only owns small watch brands and no alcohol or cosmetics brands.

These specificities express, above all, chronological differences in the involvement of these groups in the luxury goods sector. When LVMH was founded in 1987, the Louis Vuitton and Moët-Hennessy consolidation had begun a decade earlier, with a wide diversity of products from the start. Richemont and Kering invested later, in the 1990s and after 2000, respectively, based on a strong brand—Cartier for the former and Gucci for the latter—from which expansion and diversification took place. The original specialization of these two groups is still important today.

Beyond these differences, the three luxury conglomerates share many similarities. First, the role of the entrepreneurial spirit of their founders and the organization of their governance must be mentioned. LVMH (Bernard Arnault), Richemont (Anton Rupert), and Kering (François Pinault) were all created by businessmen who had seized the opportunities presented to European luxury brands in the global market at the end of the twentieth century. The strategy itself is not particularly innovative. It is basically the implementation of the three-pronged investment (production, distribution, organization) put in place by the large modern American companies during the last quarter of the nineteenth century, as analyzed by the business historian Alfred Chandler.[20] As most European luxury goods manufacturers remained small family businesses with limited resources in terms of capital and knowledge, the idea of mass-producing and mass-selling luxury goods was completely new in the 1980s. The entrepreneurs who created the luxury conglomerates came from finance, real estate, and trading, among other fields. They had organizational skills rather than the traditional knowledge of how to make the luxury goods they sold around the world. Furthermore, they could attract external investors who provided the capital necessary for the strong expansion of these conglomerates (buying up companies and setting up a global sales network). However, despite the opening up of their capital, these conglomerates all remained controlled by the founding families through the ownership of special shares that gave them preferential voting rights. Finally, in all three cases, the family character of these groups was reinforced by the involvement of second-generation representatives in operational management positions. From this perspective, it can be said that the luxury industry is now dominated by family businesses.

These three groups are then all deeply international, with strong European roots. Although two of them are headquartered in France and the third in Geneva, Switzerland, a city close to Paris, they are not French luxury companies. Their external growth, through the acquisition of companies, has led them to buy many brands across Europe (mainly in France, Italy, Britain, Switzerland, and Spain), as well as some American designer companies and some Chinese jewelry, liquor, and fashion companies. The owners and managers of the conglomerates understand that all these European brands share a common identity (traditional know-how, high quality, craftsmanship, the art of living, etc.), representing a great value on the world market. The internationalization of these groups is also illustrated by sales all over the world, with a growing share of Asia and a significant share of employment outside France—or Switzerland for Richemont.

Finally, the competitive advantage of conglomerates lies in their ability to manage key resources for their brands on a global scale. This ability is particularly evident in finance, logistics and real estate. These groups own financial companies that invest in various shopping center projects around the world and make shops available to their brands. For example, LVMH has two subsidiaries, L Capital Asia (LCA) and L Real Estate (LRE), which play a major role in the group's expansion in Asia. As for Richemont, it has the subsidiary Richemont Asia Pacific Ltd, which is particularly active in Hong Kong. These financial and logistical skills are at the heart of the conglomerates' expansion in emerging countries, particularly China.[21] They allow the opening of mono-brand stores, which contribute to improving the visibility of the brands. Between 2000 and 2014, the number of boutiques owned by the groups rose from 1,286 to 3,708 for LVMH, from 444 to 1,056 for Richemont and from 196 to 1,186 for Kering. Since 2015, the rise of internet sales has reduced the importance of boutiques, although they remain essential for showcasing the brands and educating consumers.

The second competitive advantage of conglomerates is their ability to manage creativity on a group-wide basis—a major resource for the luxury industry. The many brands that belong to conglomerates all have their own specificities in terms of products and positioning, which results in individual creative strategies. However, these are embedded in a hierarchical relationship to the conglomerates' headquarters. The strong control exercised by the head offices, through committees of managers who coordinate the activities and positioning of the brands, has several advantages. Firstly, it allows synergies and collaborations to be realized between brands operating in different sectors.[22] It is possible to use the production capabilities of one brand for another and thus expand the product range without depending on external suppliers. The launch of accessories is particularly important for high-fashion brands because they can increase the customer base and at the same time make significant profits.[23] For example, when LVMH was founded in 1987, Louis Vuitton signed a contract with Christian Lacroix, an

Figure 4.4 The luxury shopping mall L'Avenue, in Shanghai, opened in 2013, was developed by a joint venture co-founded by L Real Estate, a subsidiary of LVMH, and Hong Kong billionaire Stanley Ho.
Source: Getty Image, ID: 93589558
Credit: VCG / Contributor

haute couture house owned by Bernard Arnault, to manufacture leather goods.[24] Similarly, following the acquisition of Swiss watch companies, LVMH opened a new subsidiary in La Chaux-de-Fonds (Switzerland) in 2001 to assemble watches for Christian Dior, Fred and Louis Vuitton. In 2002, Louis Vuitton was able to launch its first collection of watches, equipped in particular with movements manufactured by Zenith, an LVMH company since 1999.[25] We observe a similar process for perfumes: the fashion brand Kenzo launched its own perfumes in 2000 before the subsidiary LVMH Fragrance Brands was created in 2010. The situation is identical in the other conglomerates. Internal synergies enabled Montblanc to launch a watch collection at the end of the 1990s, while Kering founded a subsidiary specializing in the manufacture of sunglasses.

Secondly, conglomerates have the financial capacity to invest massively in the control of their supply of raw materials and semi-finished products, which serves to reinforce their independence from their competitors. This process of verticalization by buying out subcontractors has become an essential issue in the luxury industry since 2000. Thus, in 2009, LVMH created a joint venture in Belgium, Tanneries de la Comète SA, in cooperation with Masure Tannery, a leather supplier to Louis Vuitton since 1988. Three years later, in 2012, the group bought a second tannery in the south of France.[26] This

Figure 4.5 Louis Vuitton, fashion collection, Nara, Japan, 2021.
Source: author.

consolidation process is particularly visible in the watchmaking sector, where Swatch Group, the world's leading company in this sector, has a de facto quasi-monopoly in the production and distribution of components essential to the functioning of mechanical watches (blanks, springs, etc.). Cartier and Tag Heuer, the major watch brands of the Richemont and LVMH groups, depended on the Swatch Group for their supply of movements. After the decision was taken in 2002 to gradually cease supplying its competitors, Swatch Group led its competitors to invest massively in the development of their production apparatus, notably by buying up small independent companies.[27]

In parallel with these acquisitions, the conglomerates are developing various activities to encourage the preservation of traditional know-how and independent craftsmanship, mainly through programs to support new generations of craftsmen. LVMH, through its subsidiary Loewe, opened a leather goods school in Spain (*Escuela de Maroquinería*) in 2013 and launched its Institut des Métiers d'Excellence in France the following year, which offers a series of programs in collaboration with French vocational schools, particularly in the fields of couture and jewelry. In Switzerland, Richemont is one of the major promoters of the Fondation de Haute Horlogerie (FHH), an institution created in 2005 to encourage the development of craftsmanship in the decoration of luxury watches and to promote the group's brands.[28]

Thirdly, the conglomerates, mainly LVMH and Kering, are the promoters of the transformation of Parisian haute couture into a creative and artistic activity intended to produce added value for the brands. Whereas Christian Dior designed classic dresses for the post-war upper-middle-class, his successor at the head of the company between 1996 and 2010, John Galliano, turned Dior's fashion shows into real art shows. Tom Ford at Gucci and Marc Jacobs at Louis Vuitton are other examples of luxury houses that have become established as creators of art. Their visibility is expressed during the fashion shows that reinforce the desirability of these brands on the global market— and result in rapid growth in sales of accessories and ready-to-wear. In 2000, Arnault reported that Dior's ready-to-wear sales had quadrupled since Galliano's arrival.[29] Artistic creation is, therefore, not only the result of the activity of brilliant designers. It is an essential resource, managed as such by conglomerates that retain strong control over their brands.

4.5 Conclusion

This chapter has explained how the three top luxury conglomerates, LVMH, Richemont and Kering, were founded and have developed since the 1980s. Although these groups largely dominate the modern luxury industry, they represent only one particular organizational form of the players in this sector. If we look at all the companies in the ranking of the 100 top luxury firms (Table 2.1), we can see that almost all of them are specialized in a particular type of product, such as fashion, leather goods, watches, or cosmetics.

The importance of these diversified conglomerates lies not only in their size and financial strength but also in the new marketing strategies they have implemented—see the example of Christian Dior in Chapter 3—which are becoming references for the whole industry. The mass production of luxury goods, their worldwide distribution, especially in mono-brand shops, as well as globalized advertising campaigns aimed at building strong brands, form the basis of a new business model that is now followed by most luxury companies. This new model requires abundant capital, which is why independent companies tend to go public.

CHAPTER 5
THE INDEPENDENT FAMILY
BUSINESS—ITALIAN FASHION

In 1980, the film *American Gigolo* was released and made actor Richard Gere the sex symbol of a whole generation. His plastic beauty and natural ease expressed a new incarnation of masculinity, which would lead some fifteen years later to the metrosexual. For the Italian fashion designer who dressed the American actor in this Hollywood production, it was also an opportunity to establish himself as the representative of a new elegance, less classic and more casual. Five years earlier, Giorgio Armani had opened his haute couture house in Milan and was now about to conquer the American market. He was a runaway success and became the expression of Italian fashion throughout the world.

In 2017, with a turnover of more than €2.6 billion, Giorgio Armani SpA was one of the ten top luxury fashion companies in the world and the second-largest in Italy behind the Prada group. It embodied an organizational model different from conglomerates, although it largely adopted the marketing strategy implemented by the latter (global brands, control of distribution, and democratization of consumption). Giorgio Armani SpA remains an independent company, as are many Italian firms active in fashion and textiles. It is not listed on the stock exchange, nor is it part of a conglomerate; it focuses on developing its own brands. How representative is it of the Italian fashion industry as a whole? What are the challenges of this independence?

5.1 From haute couture to fashion group: Giorgio Armani

The success of the Italian luxury fashion industry in world markets in the last third of the twentieth century, Giorgio Armani being a prime example, was due to its ability to respond to a demand for fashion that French couturiers had not anticipated. Parisian haute couture, which relied on unique creations for an exclusive clientele, was in crisis during the 1960s and 1970s, mainly because of the new behavior of wealthy consumers, who wanted simpler, easier-to-wear clothes. The number of Parisian haute couture houses fell from 106 in 1946 to only nineteen in 1967—and then 16 in 1999.[1] This crisis led French couturiers to revise their business model and intensify their presence in mass-produced clothing (prêt-à-porter) and accessories, as Christian Dior did.[2] However, it was mainly Italian and American designers who became the suppliers of casual luxury fashion.

Although the Italian textile industry had been developing strongly since the end of the nineteenth century, it was in the 1950s that fashion entered its first phase of development, based on the meeting between Italian designers and American representatives of department stores.[3] In the 1960s, Milan established itself as the capital of Italian haute

Figure 5.1 Armani Exchange store, 2017.
Source: Wikimedia Commons.
https://commons.wikimedia.org/wiki/File:ArmaniExchangeFestivalWalk.jpg

couture and set out to challenge the monopolistic position of Paris. Giorgio Armani, born in 1934 in northern Italy, began his career in the Lombardy capital.[4] In 1957, he was hired as an interior decorator and then as a menswear salesman by the department store La Rinascente, which collaborated intensively with fashion designers such as Luis Hidalgo, former artistic director of the haute couture house Biki, to develop ready-to-wear collections.[5] In 1964, Armani joined the Nina Cerruti fashion house, where he worked as a designer, before establishing himself as a freelancer in the early 1970s.

With the financial backing of his partner, businessman Sergio Galeotti, Armani set up his own company in Milan in 1975 under the name Giorgio Armani SpA. He launched his first men's fashion collection in 1976 and gradually established himself as a designer who developed both men's and women's clothing. The company quickly experienced tremendous growth thanks to its entry into the American market and its cooperation with Hollywood. From the second half of the 1970s onwards, Armani worked with showbiz stars and became one of the leading designers for Hollywood actresses. The first celebrity to attend a public event dressed by Armani was actress Diane Keaton at the 1978 Academy Awards. Many other celebrities would follow her lead in the ensuing decades, starting with the abovementioned actor, Richard Gere. Giorgio Armani was very aware of the media impact of his ambassadors. In 1986, he hired Lee Radziwill, sister of Jacqueline Kennedy Onassis and a key figure in the American jet set, as the fashion house's social events manager.[6]

Expansion into the American market was not only the result of proximity to Hollywood. Mastery of a production system was also necessary. Armani was an independent designer who did not have production capabilities when he founded his company. Gruppo Finanziario Tessile (GFT), Italy's largest manufacturer of men's clothing in the 1950s and 1970s, was responsible for the production of Armani's collections.[7] The Italian designer collaborated with GFT in the early 1970s, designing a clothing collection for them. In 1979, the two companies founded a joint venture in the United States under the name Giorgio Armani Men's Wear Corporation (later renamed Giorgio Armani Fashion Group). It was responsible for the distribution of luxury ready-to-wear in North America. GFT experienced extraordinary growth through its collaboration with Armani and other Italian fashion designers such as Valentino. Sales rose from $7 million in 1980 to 230 million in 1988. Armani's share was estimated at 20 percent of the total.[8] The expansion of sales in Asia also led GFT in 1988 to open a joint venture in China for the production of men's clothing for that part of the world.

Despite its success in luxury ready-to-wear, Armani did not allow himself to be confined to haute couture. Very early on, he seized the opportunities offered by the reputation he had acquired across the Atlantic to extend his business model to consumer fashion and accessories. In 1981, he opened a boutique in Milan that offered jeans and a range of diversified products bearing his label. His denim collection led to the creation of the Armani Jeans line, which became the basis of Emporio Armani. Accessories were mostly produced by specialized companies with whom licensing agreements were signed—for example, with L'Oréal for perfumes (1980), Luxottica for glasses (1988), and Fossil for watches (1997). The expansion into affordable fashion was accompanied by a geographical expansion, mainly into Asia. A joint venture was created in Japan in 1987 with the trading company Itochu.[9] However, the company remained firmly anchored in its traditional markets. In 2004, the Armani group's turnover was mainly generated in Italy (18 percent) and the rest of Europe (37 percent), as well as in North America (24 percent). Asia accounted for only 12 percent, and the rest of the world 9 percent.[10]

At the end of the 1980s, as the company's revenues grew through the expansion of its ranges, Armani gradually broke away from GFT and began to internalize garment production, buying up various textile companies in Italy. In particular, in 1989, he acquired a stake in his jeans manufacturer, SIM. Ten years later, in 1999, Armani owned seven factories. In 2000, he signed a cooperation agreement with his rival Ermenegildo Zegna Group for the joint management of a former GFT production center in Milan. Finally, the Italian fashion designer verticalized fashion distribution with the creation of the A/X chain of shops on the American market as a response to the meteoric rise of The Gap.[11] His first shop opened in New York, in the Soho district, in 1991. However, the concentration on jeans alone was a financial failure. At the beginning of the twenty-first century, the A/X Armani Exchange chain was repositioned as a general fast-fashion brand and introduced in Asia and Latin America.

Horizontal (various Armani lines) and vertical (design, production, marketing, sales) concentrations in the 1980s and 1990s, respectively, gave rise to a highly internalized group, which continues to grow strongly. The company's revenues rose from $306 million in 1990 to €1.6 billion in 2004 and €2.1 billion in 2018.[12] As the company is not listed on the stock exchange, it publishes little information on its turnover. However, the work of historian

Table 5.1 Armani Group turnover, in millions of euros, 2004

Brand		%	Products		%
Giorgio Armani	531,1	32	Clothing	892,2	53
Emporio Armani	428,8	26	Perfumes and cosmetics	450,5	27
Armani Collezioni	305,1	18	Glasses	130,2	8
Armani Jeans	263,2	16	Watches and jewelry	104,5	6
A/X Armani Exchange	118,6	7	Other	93,9	6
Other	24,5	1			
Total	1 671,3	100	Total	1 671,3	100

Source: Merlo, p. 353.

Elisabetta Merlo provides information on the composition of turnover in 2004 (Table 5.1), highlighting the group's balanced position in its various business segments, from haute couture (Giorgio Armani) and luxury ready-to-wear (Armani Collezioni) to consumer fashion (Emporio Armani) and fast fashion and accessories (Armani Jeans and A/X Armani Exchange). Its presence in all fashion segments was accompanied by strong product diversification, as clothing accounted for just over half of the group's sales in all segments.

While Armani's presence in all fashion segments was certainly a specific feature of the company, another characteristic was representative of the Italian luxury fashion industry as a whole: the collaboration between the textile industry and independent designers. In particular, the GFT group, which employed 5,800 people in Italy in 1978, played a key role. This company introduced the Fordist system of mass production and distribution into the production of clothing in Italy.[13] It placed its production capacity at the disposal of a new generation of designers for the production, and sometimes the distribution, of their collections. Armani, but also Valentino, Ungaro and Montana benefited from the opportunities GFT offered.[14] In the mid-1980s, GFT became the world's largest fashion producer, with a turnover of $694 million in 1987.[15] But during this same period, it began to face growing difficulties, with the global expansion of fast-fashion chains that were undercutting prices and the growth of fashion houses that, like Armani, were gradually internalizing their production capacities. GFT suffered its first loss in 1991, which led to the gradual dismantling of the group.

5.2 Characteristics of the Italian fashion industry

Is Giorgio Armani SpA, an independent, unlisted company with a turnover of over €2 billion, representative of the Italian luxury fashion industry as a whole? To answer this question, it is necessary to have a global view of the sector. There are two main ways to understand this industry: looking at the companies and looking at the brands.

Let us start with the companies. The Deloitte ranking presented in Chapter 2 identifies Italian luxury firms with a turnover of more than $200 million in 2017 (Table 2.1). There is a total of twenty-four of them, whose main activity is fashion (15), eyewear (4), footwear (3), perfumery (1), and leather goods (1). Except for the eyewear manufacturers Luxottica, Marcolin and Safilo, and the perfume manufacturer Euroitalia (which all produce accessories under license for the major luxury brands active in other sectors), the Italian companies own their own brands. Most of these companies are small (turnover of less than $500 million for eight of them; between 500 and 800 million for four others), relatively recently established (five companies founded between 1910 and 1945; six in the 1950s and 1960s; thirteen since 1970) and have retained their independence (fifteen of them are unlisted). Apart from the question of size, Giorgio Armani SpA is representative of this general trend.

Figure 5.2 Tod's store, Osaka, 2020.
Source: author.

From looking at the history and structure of these companies, we can identify three different business models. Firstly, there are large fashion and footwear houses that follow a similar trajectory to Giorgio Armani. These are Dolce & Gabbana, Salvatore Ferragamo, Prada, Valentino, Gianni Versace, and Ermenegildo Zegna. Founded and developed by independent designers, their brands benefit from the media impact of their proximity to a clientele of showbiz stars. The growth of these firms is based as much on product diversification as on the verticalization of distribution. In 2017, they all had a turnover of more than one billion dollars, except Gianni Versace, and only two are listed on the stock exchange (Salvatore Ferragamo and Prada). Leather goods manufacturer Tod's, which has been expanding its brand ranges and diversifying into fashion since the 1990s, can be included in this category.[16] These companies embody the excellence of Italian fashion in the global luxury market.

Secondly, nine small fashion companies have remained specialized in their activity: Aeffe, Brunello Cucinelli, Etro, Fashion Box, Liu Jo, Max Mara, OTB, Twinset-Simona Barbieri, and Giuseppe Zanotti. Some have bought other fashion brands and formed a group organization (OTB) or diversified into accessories. However, these external growth strategies are rare and not very developed, owing to the small size of these companies. Only three had a turnover of more than $500 million in 2017, and only one exceeded the billion-dollar mark. Only two companies are listed on the stock exchange. Most sell niche products.[17] Other companies in this category include leather goods manufacturers Furla and Moncler, which moved from sportswear to luxury fashion after 2000.[18]

Thirdly, Italy has five companies that specialize in manufacturing luxury accessories (glasses and perfumes) for major international brands (Euroitalia, Luxottica, Marcolin, De Rigo, Safilo). These are both large, listed companies, such as Luxottica and Safilo, and small, unlisted companies. They are, however, on the fringe of the model discussed here, in the sense that they are not companies specifically active in fashion. Rather they belong to the model of the diversified industrial group, discussed in the next chapter.

However, this analysis of the Italian luxury industry based on the companies that comprise this sector does not tell the whole story. French luxury conglomerates, Middle Eastern investment funds and foreign fashion groups own numerous Italian brands, acquired for the most part since the end of the 1990s in the context of the organizational transformation of the global luxury industry. To assess the importance and representativeness of these acquisitions, we need to look at the top Italian luxury brands. Table 5.2 shows the fashion brands included in the top 100 Italian brands, ranked in 2012 by MPP Consulting. There was a total of twenty-seven brands, twelve owned by foreign companies. Kering acquired three brands, LVMH two, and Richemont one. The foreign buyers also included Asian textile groups such as Fila Korea (South Korea) and Trinity (Hong Kong), the American fashion group Michael Kors, and investment funds from Qatar (Mayhoola for Investments), and Dubai (Vision Investment and Paris Group). Remarkably, Italian companies were almost absent among the buyers. Aeffe did buy Moschino, and Prada also owns the Miu Miu brand, but these are exceptions.

The analysis of the Italian luxury industry thus allows us to highlight some ideal types of firms: the large, diversified luxury firm, the small fashion firm, and the firm acquired

Table 5.2 Fashion brands among the top 100 Italian brands in 2012

Brand	Value (million dollars)	Current owner and date of acquisition
Prada	5 752	Independent, listed
Giorgio Armani	4 597	Independent, unlisted
Gucci	4 428	Kering (1999)
Bulgari	2 344	LVMH (2011)
Dolce & Gabbana	2 301	Independent, unlisted
Chicco	1 646	Independent, unlisted
Benetton	1 221	Independent, unlisted
Diesel	1 103	Independent, unlisted
Versace	795	Michael Kors (2018)
Moschino	553	Aeffe (1999)
Valentino	532	Mayhoola for Investments SPC (2002)
Fila	487	Fila Korea (2007)
Salvatore Ferragamo	455	Independent, listed
Fendi	413	LVMH (2001)
Mandarina Duck	380	Independent, unlisted
Lotto	363	Independent, unlisted
Brioni	306	Kering (2012)
Miu Miu	291	Prada Group
Diadora	283	Independent, unlisted
Roberto Cavalli	234	Vision Investment Co. (2019)
Gianfranco Ferré	199	Paris Group (2011)
Cerruti 1881	192	Trinity Ltd (2010)
Ermenegildo Zegna	173	Independent, unlisted
Kappa	155	Independent, unlisted
GAS	149	Independent, unlisted
Bottega Veneta	142	Kering (2001)
Officine Panerai	119	Richemont (1997)

Source: MPP Consulting.

by a foreign group. The case studies that follow illustrate the trajectories followed by firms belonging to these various models. They highlight the factors that contribute (or not) to the pursuit of independent development.

5.3 A large, diversified luxury company: Ermenegildo Zegna

The ten or so large Italian luxury companies include relatively recent ones (i.e., founded in the last third of the twentieth century, such as Giorgio Armani, Dolce & Gabbana, and Gianni Versace) and older companies that have positioned themselves in the luxury market during the same period, such as Ermenegildo Zegna, whose development is analyzed below.

Ermenegildo Zegna ($1.4 billion in revenue in 2017) began in textile production in the late nineteenth century.[19] The company was founded in 1889 by Angelo Zegna and specialized in wool weaving. It was one of the many textile companies on which the Italian industrial revolution was based. Taken over in 1910 by Ermenegildo Zegna, the founder's youngest son, it developed as a supplier of woolen fabrics for the fashion industry and registered the Zegna brand in 1939. The transition to a luxury fashion company took place in two stages. In the first stage, Zegna abandoned its status as a specialist subcontractor and began producing men's ready-to-wear clothing (1968) and then tailoring (1972). It opened its first mono-brand store in Paris in 1980 and Milan in 1985. In the second phase, Zegna adopted a strategy characterized by global expansion (opening of a boutique in Beijing in 1991), the internalization of the production of high-quality products (acquisition of the wool manufacturer Agnona SpA in 2000 and the leather goods manufacturer Longhi in 2002), product diversification through licensing agreements (with L'Oréal, Marcolin Group and Girard-Perregaux), the creation of joint ventures (ZeFer co-founded in 2002 with Salvatore Ferragamo for the production of shoes) and equity investments (50 percent of the capital of the Chinese luxury fashion company Shar Moon, in 2003). Finally, in 2003, it launched a second brand, Z Zegna, aimed at a younger and less wealthy clientele. The maintenance and development of its production capacity for luxury goods enabled it to supply some of the big names in fashion that had no, or limited, production capacities, such as Gucci, Yves Saint Laurent, and Tom Ford. Between 1990 and 2019, Zegna underwent a profound transformation, marked by strong vertical integration and product diversification. However, the company remained a family business. It is not listed on the stock exchange and is developing steadily, which suggests growth is based on self-financing. Its turnover amounted to approximately $350 million in 1990,[20] and it was valued at €601 million in 2003 and €963 million in 2010.[21] The desire to maintain family control over the firm, no doubt, explains why Zegna did not become a diversified luxury group but remained essentially focused on its own brand. The transition from specialized production to a marketing position—the excellence of Italian style and wool work—was based on heritage strategies that allowed strong and coherent discourses for the global market.

Figure 5.3 Ermenegildo Zegna store, Paris, 2014.
Source: Getty Image, ID: 477014151
Credit: Michel Dufour / Contributor

5.4 A small specialist fashion company: Aeffe

Small fashion companies, mostly founded after 1970, make up almost half of Italian luxury companies. As they are usually family-owned and not listed on the stock exchange, little is known of the evolution of their management or their international development. It is hard to assess to what extent they adopted the general model of transformation of the global luxury industry at the end of the twentieth century (financialization, internationalization, and democratization). The presence of Aeffe on the stock exchange does, however, provide access to figures that express the development of this independent firm.[22]

The Aeffe Group is a company specializing in the manufacture and distribution of clothing. It was founded in the mid-1970s by fashion designer Alberta Ferretti to produce her ready-to-wear collections, remaining specialized until the end of the 1990s and, since 1983, producing clothes under license for the designer Franco Moschino. The first phase of expansion took place at the turn of the twenty-first century with the takeover of the fashion brands Moschino (1999) and Velmar (2001), as well as the leather goods company Pollini (2001). Aeffe became a small Italian fashion group. Its growth required capital raising, achieved with the listing on the Milan Stock Exchange in 2007. The company also manufactures clothing under license for designers such as Jean-Paul Gaultier and

Emanuel Ungaro. However, despite the IPO, the Ferretti family remains the main shareholder (38 percent of the capital in 2019 held by Fratelli Ferretti Holding) and continues to run the firm. The firm did not see its business model change fundamentally after 2000. On the contrary, the traditional model was consolidated. Between 2004 and 2019, turnover grew slightly from €251 million to 362 million, based on the expansion of traditional markets (Italy from 39 percent to 46 percent of sales, and the rest of Europe from 20 percent to 25 percent) and a small increase in retail sales (19 percent in 2004 and 27 percent in 2019).

Thus, Aeffe presents the case of a small family firm whose owners limit development in order to retain control. Going public is not in contradiction to typical Italian family capitalism.[23] However, this small fashion company does not have the capital to create a French-style conglomerate. Without a media designer-founder, such as Armani, or a particular historical experience, such as Zegna, it is hard to adopt a legacy strategy to build strong brands in the global luxury market. Smaller companies such as Aeffe are, therefore, often the target of external investors.

5.5 The failure of Italian family capitalism: Gucci and Bulgari

Finally, it is worth examining the case of Italian luxury companies taken over by foreign groups to shed light on the conditions under which these takeovers occurred. This section looks at the examples of Gucci and Bulgari, two family-owned companies that were originally specialized—the former in leather goods and the latter in jewelry—and that underwent strong expansion (product diversification and market expansion) in the last decades of the twentieth century but whose capital requirements challenged their independent organization.

Gucci has its origins in a small, high-end leather goods business opened in Florence in 1923 by Guccio Gucci.[24] It was a classic luxury business, producing and selling exclusive goods to the upper-middle class. After the Second World War, the founder's three sons continued the business. In the early 1950s, they moved to the United States, led by Aldo Gucci, where they became suppliers of leather accessories and footwear to Hollywood stars and the American jet set. Building on this reputation, the Gucci brothers began a major expansion into the American market, and then into Europe. They opened boutiques and issued licenses for accessories. By 1979, Gucci reportedly owned a collection of 20,000 products bearing its label, including liquor, condoms, and toilet paper.[25] Under these conditions, it was no longer possible to maintain the brand's glamorous and luxurious image. Gucci is a textbook case of the decline in the value of a luxury brand through excessive democratization through multiple licenses. During the 1980s, the company was also plagued by family conflicts and tax evasion. Unable to reform, it could not adopt a new strategy to re-establish itself as a luxury brand with the public. The American subsidiary lost money in the early 1990s and went into debt. In 1992–3, the Gucci family sold the company to the Investcorp investment fund. Established in Bahrain in 1982, this fund specialised in buying, restructuring, and selling troubled luxury companies, such as the American jeweler Tiffany and the Swiss watchmaker Breguet.[26]

In this context, a new management team was appointed in 1994. The Italian lawyer and businessman Domenico De Sole, former legal advisor to Gucci in the United States who became CEO of Gucci America in 1984, took over the operational management of the group. He was assisted by the American designer Tom Ford, who was appointed artistic director of the brand. The two men repositioned Gucci as a luxury brand in the second half of the 1990s, drastically reducing the number of licenses (from 20,000 to 7,000 products between 1995 and 1999), taking over the Gucci boutiques and launching new haute couture collections. The personality of Tom Ford, who not only embodied the brand but was himself a media celebrity comparable to John Galliano at Dior,[27] contributed to this success. Turnover rose from around $500 million in 1986 to 2.3 billion in 2000.[28] Such growth whets the appetite. Initially, it was Investcorp that reaped the benefits of its investment, with the listing of 30 percent of the capital in 1995 and the sale of the balance in 1997. In a second phase, luxury conglomerates seized the opportunity of Gucci's presence on the financial market to take control. Prada acquired almost 10 percent of Gucci's shares, which were quickly sold to LVMH. Bernard Arnault controlled 34 percent of the capital in 1999, which fueled the fears of the Italian managers, who wanted to retain their autonomy. His rival PPR (Kering since 2005) then made an agreement with Gucci: a capital increase allowed PPR to control 40 percent of Gucci while LVMH's share was reduced to 20

Figure 5.4 Aldo Gucci, at the opening of his new shop at Bond Street, London, 1977.
Source: Getty Image, ID: 3396076
Credit: John Minihan / Stringer

percent. The dispute between the two French giants continued in court, and it was PPR that ultimately took control of Gucci in 2001, making it the core of its luxury division.[29]

Bulgari is a family-owned jewelry company that diversified into luxury accessories in the late twentieth century.[30] Its origins date back to the last third of the nineteenth century when a Greek goldsmith named Sotirio Boulgaris settled in Rome. He Italianized his name to Bulgari and opened a shop in the Italian capital in 1884, where he sold his creations (jewelry and tableware). The family business grew over the decades and established itself as one of Italy's leading jewelers, whose products were inspired by art and architecture rather than nature, setting them apart from their French and American competitors.

It was the third generation of management that embarked on a strategy of international expansion and product diversification. First, a shop was opened in 1970 in New York on Fifth Avenue, followed by boutiques in Geneva, Monaco and Paris in the years that followed. Then, in 1975, a subsidiary was opened in Switzerland under the name Bulgari Brothers (renamed Time in the early 1980s) to oversee the supply of lighters, pens, and watches.[31] There was clearly a desire to emulate Cartier, which had undertaken a similar strategy a few years earlier. In 1977, the Italian jeweler launched the Bvlgari-Bvlgari watch, designed by the famous Geneva watch designer Gérald Genta.[32] Despite this expansion, the company remained small, its turnover estimated at 50 million dollars in the late 1970s.[33]

The real turning point came in 1985. The stagnation of the business and conflicts between the Bulgari brothers who ran the family firm led them to call a representative of the fourth generation, their nephew Francesco Trapani, to take charge of and revitalize the family firm. Francesco Trapani undertook a profound transformation, typical of the luxury houses of the period. He repositioned Bulgari, previously aimed primarily at the upper-middle-class, as an accessible luxury brand and opened a series of boutiques in the world's major cities in the second half of the 1980s. Diversification into luxury accessories also accelerated. Bulgari opened a watch factory in Neuchâtel, Switzerland, in 1990.[34] It launched perfume collections, silk accessories, leather goods, and eyewear. All it needed was a clothing line to establish itself as a generalist luxury manufacturer. Trapani's strategy was successful. Bulgari's turnover reached $150 million in 1989 and 269 million in 1996.

However, the continuation of this growth model requires significant investments. In 1995, Bulgari was listed on the Milan Stock Exchange and offered 32 percent of its capital to investors. But Trapani expressed his desire to remain independent. In 2001, he stated that "independent companies have grown faster than medium-sized brands integrated into large groups, which have gone nowhere."[35] He continued his all-out diversification into porcelain (licensing agreement with the German manufacturer Rosenthal in 1998), his consolidation in mechanical watchmaking with great complications (takeover of the Swiss companies Gérald Genta SA and Daniel Roth SA in 1999) and the hotel industry (creation of a joint venture with Marriott International in 2001).[36] The turnover reached €766 million in 2000 and 1.1 billion in 2010.[37] In March 2011, Bernard Arnault announced the acquisition of Bulgari by LVMH. This operation allowed him to strengthen his jewelry division to face Cartier and Tiffany.[38] Bulgari needed to increase its capital to continue its global expansion. However, the family only controlled 51 percent of the company's capital at the time and could not continue to open up the company and risk losing control. Hence, Trapani preferred to negotiate the conditions of its integration into a conglomerate. The Bulgari family received 3.5 percent of the capital of LVMH in exchange for their company, making them the second-largest family shareholder in the luxury group. As for Trapani, he was appointed a member of the LVMH board of directors and president of the watch and jewelry division, a position he held until 2014.

The cases of Gucci and Bulgari illustrate perfectly that the takeover of independent family businesses by conglomerates is not simply the result of intrinsic weaknesses in such firms. It is also worth highlighting the fierce competition between the luxury giants in their race to build a portfolio of diversified and complementary brands. The case of jewelry, briefly discussed with Bulgari, is an excellent expression of this. Except for Chopard and Graff, all the main luxury jewelry brands today belong to conglomerates.[39] In 1999, Compagnie Financière Richemont, the most powerful conglomerate in jewelry, acquired the Franco-American company Van Cleef & Arpels, then owned by the Italian textile group Frateni, and in 2019, the Italian jeweler Buccellati, a goldsmith distinguished by Renaissance-inspired jewels. These are niche products that complement the two flagship brands that Richemont has owned since its foundation: Cartier and Piaget. As for LVMH, absent from this sector at its foundation, it took control of Fred Joaillier in 1995, a small French brand essentially positioned in the domestic market, followed by the takeover of another French house, Chaumet (1999), the creation of a joint venture with the South African diamond dealer De Beers for the commercial exploitation of this brand for the sale of mounted diamonds (2001) and the takeover of Bulgari (2011). However, De

Figure 5.5 Bulgari flagship store, Via Condotti, Rome, 2018.
Source: Wikimedia Commons.
https://commons.wikimedia.org/wiki/File:Bvlgari2.jpg?uselang=fr

Beers failed to gain a foothold in the coveted fine jewelry market, and LVMH withdrew from the joint venture in 2017 before announcing the takeover of Tiffany two years later. The example of the competition between Richemont and LVMH to build up portfolios of jewelry brands shows how conglomerates do more than rescue struggling independent family businesses: they invest considerable sums in their acquisitions for strategic reasons.

5.6 Conclusion

Giorgio Armani SpA is, therefore, representative of only one part of the Italian luxury fashion industry, one that has managed to grow in the global market while remaining independent. This model, which includes big names such as Ferragamo, Prada, and Zegna, is characterized by self-financing, stable growth, a strong heritage usually based on the charisma of the founder and strongly integrated activities (accessories, various clothing lines, distribution). Outside Italy, several single-product companies have also managed to maintain their independence—for example, Chanel in haute couture, Hermès, and Longchamp in leather goods and accessories, Pandora and Swarovski in premium jewelry, and Rolex, Patek Philippe, and Audemars Piguet in watches. They share a set of specific characteristics (financial independence, absence of major family conflicts, strong brands based on the exploitation of iconic products) in common with the Italian luxury couturiers that have allowed them to grow in the global market without integration within conglomerates.

The success story of Armani and the abovementioned firms does not mean, however, that all independent companies have followed this model. In the Italian fashion industry, there are, first of all, the small, specialized companies founded in the last quarter of the twentieth century. Their small size, niche position and lack of a specific heritage strategy—their main message is based on the expression *Made in Italy*—have limited their development. These factors make them prime targets for investors wishing to own Italian companies in their portfolio of luxury brands.

The takeover of Italian family-owned luxury companies by foreign groups is certainly a characteristic of this industry. The cases of Gucci and Bulgari present distinct trajectories in many respects, notably in terms of product diversification (strong for the first, limited for the second) and level of growth (very strong for the first, stable for the second) during the 1960s and 1970s. However, during the 1980s, both faced financial (stagnation of turnover and/or debt) and managerial (family conflicts) difficulties that led their owners to appoint new managers in order to implement a growth strategy for the globalised luxury market. This policy of repositioning—more a continuity for Armani and the other independent Italian fashion houses—implies financial means that the founding families do not have, or do not want, to invest, providing an opportunity for a takeover by Kering and LVMH.

The limits of traditional family capitalism in a globalized luxury market are not unique to Italy. We can see the same phenomenon in fashion and champagne in France and watchmaking in Switzerland, where conglomerates or industrial groups have taken over many independent family businesses. However, this raises the question: why have no diversified luxury groups or conglomerates emerged in Italy? The Benetton family made one of the few attempts. After experiencing tremendous growth in the knitwear market during the 1970s and 1980s, it tried to reinvest its profits in the fashion house Fiorucci (1981) and purchase the high-end shoe manufacturer Calzaturificio di Varese (1984). But this diversification proved unsuccessful because of the difficulties encountered in trying to unify small companies with strong identities.[40]

Elisabetta Merlo explains these difficulties by what she calls the limits of Italian capitalism: privately owned companies belonging to families who want to keep their independence but are undercapitalized, making them ideal targets for acquisition by foreign groups. Rivalries between the various family-owned companies in the luxury industry have diminished their ability to cooperate.[41] The luxury management guru Jean-Noël Kapferer and the French business press have a similar view.[42]

However, we need to think beyond the luxury industry itself. The large French and Swiss conglomerates were set up by entrepreneurs from other industries who seized the opportunities offered by traditional luxury brands in a market undergoing radical change. It is all the more surprising that no Italian entrepreneur took the opportunity to create a luxury group, as companies with a pyramid-shaped organizational structure, such as LVMH, are commonplace in Italy.[43] The abovementioned attempt by the Benetton brothers came precisely from entrepreneurs from the fashion industry. This lack of entrepreneurship is similar in Britain, where a big name in fashion (Burberry) and many independent designer brands (such as Paul Smith and Alexander McQueen) have not encouraged British entrepreneurs to form a conglomerate.

CHAPTER 6
INDUSTRIAL GROUPS

In 1994, Audi launched its top-of-the-range A8 sedan and made a striking entry into the German premium car market, which had previously been dominated by Mercedes-Benz and BMW. The operation aimed at a profound transformation of the Audi brand, perceived at the time as targeted at middle-aged men. The firm's managers developed an innovative product (a powerful car with an aluminum body), identified a new target (high-income consumers, including families and women) and adopted a marketing strategy inspired by luxury (exclusive services for customers, specific distribution network etc.).[1] Success was rapid. While sales had stagnated at around 400,000 cars per year since 1985, almost half of which were in the domestic market, they rose to over 653,000 vehicles in 2000 (63.3 percent abroad) and to over 1.8 million per year between 2015 and 2019 (85 percent abroad).[2]

Audi's transformation into an affordable luxury brand in the automotive market was not only the result of the new strategy implemented in the mid-1990s. A key factor contributing to its success was its integration into the Volkswagen Group. This integration allowed it to benefit from the collective platform used to produce cars for the various brands in the group. Together with Toyota, the German company is the largest car manufacturer in the world. It has built itself on internal growth, as well as on the acquisition of several competitors, such as Seat (1986), Skoda (1994), Bentley (1998), Bugatti (1998), Lamborghini (1998) and Porsche (2012). The aim is clearly to ensure a presence in all market segments, from low-cost cars to exclusive luxury cars, through the ownership of strong brands in each of them. In addition, during the 1990s, the Volkswagen group rationalized its production system towards standardization of components and a common platform for the various brands to manufacture cars.[3] Audi thus benefited from a technological and production environment that was the source of its competitive advantage in the premium market. The situation is similar for some Bentley, Lamborghini, and Porsche models, although the positioning of these brands in the exclusive luxury segment allows them to continue production independently.

From the perspective of the modern luxury industry, Volkswagen thus presents a particular type of company. Unlike diversified conglomerates such as LVMH, whose brands—or the overwhelming majority of its brands—are positioned in luxury, the German car manufacturer is not specialized in this field. Its competitive advantage does not lie in possessing a diversified and complementary portfolio of luxury brands but in the mastery of a system of development and production of industrial products on a global scale. Technological know-how is applied to a range of products positioned in the different market segments, from entry-level (Skoda) and mass-market (Volkswagen) to affordable (Audi) and exclusive (Bentley, Bugatti, Porsche, and Lamborghini) luxury.

Image 6.1 Audi A8, model L D5, 2017.
Source: Wikimedia Commons
https://commons.wikimedia.org/wiki/File:Audi_A8_L_D5_IMG_0066.jpg

The case of Audi and Volkswagen is far from unique in the car industry. For example, the Italian manufacturer Fiat, which has controlled Ferrari since the early 1970s, successively took over Alfa Romeo (1986) and Maserati (1993), while Jaguar was bought by Ford (1989) and sold to the Indian group Tata (2008), and BMW acquired Rolls Royce (1998). Mercedes-Benz is integrated into the Daimler automotive group. Of the major luxury car brands, only Aston Martin remains independent. Toyota is also an exception, in the sense that it launched its own luxury subsidiary, Lexus (1989). This wave of mergers and acquisitions, which included the entry and mid-range brands, resulted from the increasing competition on the world market after the liberalization of trade and investment. This change led the major car manufacturers to set up a globalized organization of production and to introduce a common platform for several brands. This rationalization of production, in turn, led to the formation of groups through the acquisition of independent brands.[4]

The presence in the luxury market of industrial groups active in a wide variety of segments is not unusual. The automobile industry is no exception. The hotel industry is another example. Alongside a few large American groups specializing in luxury, such as Marriott and Hyatt, some companies developed a presence in all market segments. Cases in point are the Hilton and Accor groups. The latter owns the luxury hotels Raffles and Sofitel and the premium hotels Mövenpick and Swissôtel, as well as the more accessible hotel chains Novotel and entry-level Ibis. The competitive advantage of diversified hotel groups is not technological, as in the automobile industry. It is based on the principle of offering a diversified set of services to meet all the needs of a clientele made captive by membership in loyalty programs (from a business stay in a luxury hotel to a family holiday in a low-cost hotel).[5]

Several of the world's leading luxury companies, according to the Deloitte ranking, are industrial groups, such as Swatch Group, Estée Lauder, L'Oréal, and Luxottica. What these companies have in common is that, like Volkswagen, they were not originally manufacturers of luxury goods. They are leaders in their field because of their mastery of production technologies and their ability to develop innovative products. These competitive advantages allow them to engage in the luxury industry in various ways. Swatch Group followed a similar trajectory to Volkswagen, characterized by the rationalization of the production of watch movements and the acquisition of complementary watch brands during the 1990s. The possession of one of the world's largest and most sophisticated watch-production facilities, together with the independent watch manufacturer Rolex and the Japanese watchmaker Seiko, has enabled Swatch Group to develop a portfolio of brands active in the various segments of the watch market, from entry-level (Swatch) to exclusive luxury (Blancpain and Breguet), as well as premium (Longines) and accessible luxury (Omega). I have had the opportunity to analyze the history of its development in a previous book to which I refer the reader who wishes to know more.[6]

The examples of Volkswagen and Swatch Group share similarities owing to their presence in mechanical sectors that create production synergies. The situation is significantly different for the perfumery and cosmetics and eyewear sectors, which are discussed in detail below. L'Oréal illustrates a case that is relatively similar to the automotive and watch industries, where it is specific know-how that makes growth in the luxury market possible. As for Luxottica and Interparfums, they also represent specialized industrial groups mastering specific technologies that are essential, if not exclusive, to the luxury market. They operate as subcontractors to brands in other sectors for which they produce accessories.

6.1 A giant in the cosmetics industry: L'Oréal

In 2020, L'Oréal was one of the largest companies listed on the Paris Stock Exchange in terms of capitalization, behind LVMH. It is a global company, employing in 2019 more than 66 percent of its workforce in Europe, with a good balance of sales between Western Europe (27.7 percent), North America (25.2 percent), Asia-Pacific (32.3 percent), and the rest of the world (14.8 percent). With sales of $31.8 billion, it is also considered the largest company in the global beauty market, ahead of Unilever ($22.4 billion), Estée Lauder ($14.2 billion), Procter & Gamble ($13.2 billion), and Shiseido ($9.7 billion).[7] Its leadership is based on its presence in all major segments of the beauty market. In 2019, L'Oréal had a total of thirty-six brands divided into four major divisions: consumer products (such as L'Oréal, Garnier, or Maybelline), luxury products, professional products (such as L'Oréal Professionnel or Kérastase), and skincare products (such as La Roche Posay and Laboratoires Vichy). L'Oréal is, therefore, not a company specializing in luxury goods, and its entry into this market was achieved through company acquisitions and licensing agreements fifty years after the firm was founded.

The origins of L'Oréal can be traced to a small company founded in 1909 under the name Société Française de Teintures Inoffensives Pour Cheveux to produce and market an innovation developed by Eugène Schueller (1881–1957), a chemist of Alsatian origin.[8] L'Oréal was, therefore, initially the brand name for a new dye sold in Parisian hairdressing salons. During the interwar period, the company diversified into the development of soaps, through the acquisition of Monsavon in 1928 (sold to Procter & Gamble in 1961), as well as shampoo and sunscreen through internal innovations. The company was transformed into a public limited company in 1939 under the name L'Oréal SA. After the Second World War, it continued to grow in the domestic cosmetics market and expanded abroad, particularly in the United States. It took over Laboratoires Vichy in 1955. Two years later, on the death of Schueller, the management of the firm was handed over to a professional manager from outside the family, François Dalle (1918–2005), while the founder's sole heir, his daughter Liliane Bettencourt (1922–2017), retained control of the capital. Although listed on the Paris Stock Exchange in 1963, the Bettencourt family kept control of the company through a system of preference shares and an agreement in 1974 with the Swiss multinational Nestlé, which invested in the firm. In 2019, the Bettencourt family and Nestlé owned a combined total of 56 percent of the capital.[9] The funds raised by the IPO were used to acquire numerous companies during the 1960s and 1970s.

As head of L'Oréal until 1984, Dalle transformed the small family business into a global cosmetics giant. Five years after his departure, in 1989, it was the second-largest cosmetics manufacturer in the world, behind Unilever.[10] The new strategy implemented was based on the internationalization of sales, the creation of a portfolio of complementary brands precisely positioned in the market (notably in specific sales networks), and the introduction of a multidivisional organization arranged by product and inspired by a report carried out by the American consulting firm McKinsey in 1969.[11] L'Oréal also stands out for its massive investment in advertising. The global competition between the cosmetics giants led to a veritable advertising blitz in magazines and on radio and television. In 1980, L'Oréal was considered the French company with the largest advertising budget.[12]

It was in this context of strong growth that L'Oréal entered the luxury segment. In 1965, it acquired Lancôme, a small company specializing in luxury cosmetics and perfumery. The brand became known worldwide. In 1955, it was already sold in ninety-eight countries and promoted by celebrities who acted as ambassadors. However, these were traditional luxury markets—that is, small and aimed at the upper-middle class.[13] During the 1980s, L'Oréal turned it into an accessible luxury brand aimed at a wide range of customers, which was particularly successful in the American market and then in China after its introduction in 1999.[14] This acquisition also led to the internalization of competences in perfumery which made it possible to sign a significant number of licenses with haute couture brands, such as Guy Laroche (1965), Courrèges (1970), and Cacharel (1975). During the next decade, the licensing strategy became more international, with contracts with Ralph Lauren (1985) and Giorgio Armani (1988). L'Oréal thus established itself as a potential partner of the luxury industry for the development of cosmetic accessories, as did the company Interparfums at the same time.[15] The brand portfolio expanded with the acquisition of Yves Saint Laurent Beauté, a subsidiary of PPR (2008), as well as the multiplication of licenses—for example, with Viktor & Rolf (2002), Diesel (2006), and Proenza Schouler (2015). Finally, the importance

Image 6.2 Lancôme advertising on a tramway, Hong Kong, 2018.
Source: Wikimedia Commons.
https://commons.wikimedia.org/wiki/File:HK_Tramways_11_at_Cleverly_Street_(20181202134339).jpg

and specificities of the Asian markets led to the acquisition of a stake in and then the purchase of the Japanese luxury makeup manufacturer Shu Uemura Cosmetics (2003) and the Chinese cosmetics manufacturer Yue Sai (2004).[16]

Luxury was always an ancillary business for L'Oréal, but it became an increasingly important part of the business in the early twenty-first century. Until 1999, the luxury brands were not grouped in a single division but split between a Perfumes and Beauty division (which did not have only luxury brands) and a Luxury, Dermatology, and Pharmaceuticals division. A reorganization in 2000 brought the luxury brands together into their own division, headed by Gilles Weil, former head of the Perfumes and Beauty division. This empowerment of luxury highlights the importance that it had taken on for the group.[17] An industrial reorganization was also implemented in 2009, with the regrouping of all the production sites of the luxury brands in the north of France.[18] The evolution of sales over the last twenty years clearly shows the contribution of the L'Oréal Luxe division to the company's growth (Figure 6.1). After a first decade marked by the low overall growth of the group (€12.7 billion in 2000 and €17.5 billion in 2009) and a decrease in the share of luxury goods, which fell from 26.7 percent of sales in 2000 to less than 24 percent in 2007–9, the company entered a phase of strong growth with record sales of €29.9 billion in 2019, an increase of more than 70 percent in ten years. The luxury division was a major contributor to this growth, with a 36.9 percent share in 2019. The recent growth of the L'Oréal Luxe division made the French cosmetics giant the seventh-largest luxury company in the world in 2017, according to Deloitte's ranking.

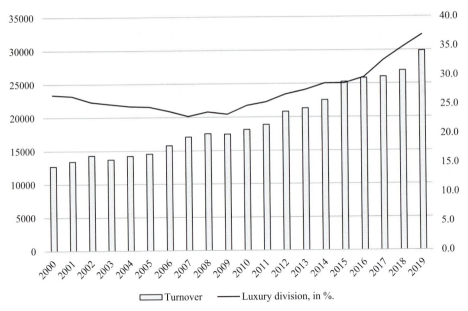

Figure 6.1 L'Oréal SA sales, in million euros, and share of the Luxury Division, in %, 2000–19.
Source: L'Oréal SA, *Annual Report*, 2000–19.

6.2 A producer of luxury accessories: Luxottica

The case of L'Oréal highlights the importance of the know-how that a firm possesses when entering and growing in the luxury market. It allowed licensing contracts with high fashion brands that wanted to have their own cosmetics. In the context of the great transformation of the 1980s and 1990s, most luxury companies adopted a strategy of diversifying into accessories to broaden their customer base and increase their profits. This opportunity was also seized by small companies that found their way to growth by specializing in the development and production of accessories for the major luxury brands. However, most of them did not build their own brands. Cases in point are several small Italian companies active in eyewear and leather goods. Some of them also started to distribute these accessories worldwide, mainly through multi-brand outlets. Among them, Luxottica SpA is undoubtedly the best example.[19]

Luxottica was originally a small eyewear frame factory, founded in the Veneto region in 1961 by Leonardo Del Vecchio, a designer born in Milan in 1935. Until the end of the 1970s, the company focused on improving production technologies, working both as a subcontractor and as an independent eyewear supplier, with the Luxottica brand being registered in 1967. The 1980s marked the first turning point. The company began to verticalize distribution on an international scale. It bought out several of its distributors and opened numerous sales subsidiaries abroad. Luxottica also began producing licensed eyewear, with the first contract being with Giorgio Armani in 1988, followed by others with the fashion designers Valentino and Yves Saint Laurent. The company was extremely successful: its turnover rose from 16 billion lire in 1979 (about $19 million) to 460 billion lire in 1991 (about $370 million).[20]

In 1990, Luxottica was listed on the New York Stock Exchange and offered 23 percent of its capital to the public, allowing the founder's family to retain control. The growth strategy was based on two main elements: investment in retail and the expansion of licenses. Until then, Luxottica had relied primarily on independent opticians to sell its eyewear; its sales network in the United States included about 28,000 opticians in the early 1990s. In 1995, Luxottica bought United States Shoe Corporation, which owned a chain of over 700 eyewear shops (LensCrafters), for $1.8 billion. The effect of this acquisition was a doubling of sales (Figure 6.2). The company continued to acquire retailers around the world after 2000. In 2018, it had over 7,000 directly operated shops. In the same year, direct sales accounted for 64 percent of turnover.

Production under license expanded considerably with the signing of contracts with Bulgari (1997), Chanel (1999), Prada (2003), Versace (2003), Donna Karan (2005), Dolce & Gabbana (2006), Burberry (2006), Polo Ralph Lauren (2007), Paul Smith (2007), Tiffany (2008), and Coach (2012). The brand portfolio was expanded with the acquisition of Ray-Ban (1999), Oakley (2007), Alain Mikli International (2013), and Fukui Megane (2018). As a result, Luxottica currently has eyewear manufacturers in Italy, the United States, France, and Japan.

As a result, Luxottica has experienced tremendous growth since the mid-1990s, with sales rising from €190 million in 1990 to 2.4 billion in 2000, reaching a peak of 9.2 billion

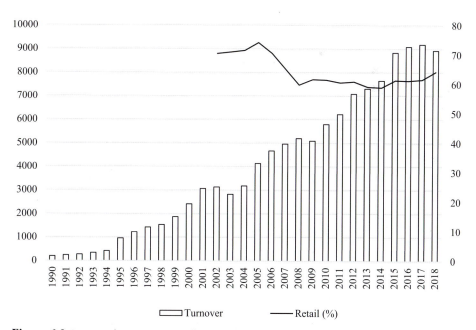

Figure 6.2 Luxottica's turnover in million euros and retail share in %, 1990–2018.
Source: Luxottica, *Annual Reports*.

in 2017 before declining slightly. In 2018, the company merged its operations with those of French company Essilor, which is active in the same field, to create a global giant with more than €15 billion in sales. Del Vecchio, Luxottica's founder, retained a decisive influence with more than 38 percent of the capital of the Luxottica-Essilor holding company at its creation.

6.3 The challenge of perfumery and the rise of Interparfums

Perfume is an ancient luxury good that accompanied the development of Parisian haute couture.[21] Pierre Guerlain opened his house in Paris in 1828. At the beginning of the 20th century, some fashion designers launched their own perfumes, a practice that boomed during the interwar period, notably with Chanel's famous N°5.[22] Some fashion houses, which had in-house perfume production capacity, sold off these profitable divisions during the 1960s and 1970s in the context of the haute couture crisis. The company Parfums Christian Dior was gradually sold to Moët & Chandon.

Since the 1980s and 1990s, perfume has become a major accessory in the global expansion strategy of luxury companies. It is a product with high added value, accessible to a mass of consumers and used to convey the message of the brands. Perfumery was, therefore, a fast-growing market at the beginning of the twenty-first century. According to the consulting firm Euromonitor International, the value of the global market grew from $33.9 billion in 2005 to 51.4 billion in 2018, with a constant share of premium and luxury brands (around 35 percent).[23] In 2018, the ten largest companies in the sector had a combined share of 56.8 percent of the global market (Table 6.1). There are, then, more than a hundred firms with small market shares. The ranking of companies does not distinguish between luxury and consumer perfumery. However, the brand data show that it is the luxury segment that allows for most of this dominance. In 2018, Coty had licenses for Calvin Klein, Hugo Boss, and Gucci, among others; L'Oréal for Giorgio Armani, Yves Saint Laurent, Lancôme, and Ralph Lauren; Puig for Paco Rabanne and Jean Paul Gaultier; and Shiseido for Dolce & Gabbana. As for Chanel and LVMH, they develop fragrances for their own brands. The ranking also includes two Brazilian cosmetics companies positioned in the mid-range.

This ranking shows that the luxury perfumery industry is dominated by two types of companies. Firstly, there are firms that are not specialized in this activity but possess a perfume production capacity. This is, of course, the LVMH group, which is vertically integrated into the perfume industry. When founded, the conglomerate controlled Parfums Dior and Parfums Givenchy. It soon took over the specialist perfumer Guerlain (1994) and the largest French perfume and cosmetics retail chain, Sephora (1997). The group's production capacity is also made available to other LVMH brands, such as Kenzo or Loewe, giving rise to a specialized subsidiary, LVMH Fragrance Brands (2011). Finally, the group continues to acquire specialist perfumers, such as Francis Kurkdjian (2017). Another example is the haute couture house Chanel SA. The production of the famous Chanel N°5 was entrusted in 1923 to a separate company, Parfums Chanel SA,

Table 6.1 Top ten global fragrance companies, market share in %, 2018

Name	Country	Main activity	Market share, in %
Coty Inc.	United States	Perfumery	11,1
L'Oréal	France	Cosmetics	8,2
LVMH	France	Diversified conglomerate	7,2
Puig SL	Spain	Cosmetics	7,1
Estée Lauder	United States	Cosmetics	5,3
Chanel SA	France	Fashion	4,5
Natura & Co.	Brazil	Cosmetics	4,2
Grupo Boticario	Brazil	Cosmetics	3,7
Avon Products	United States	Perfumery	3,3
Shiseido Co.	Japan	Cosmetics	2,2
Total			56,8 %

Source: Euromonitor International.

majority-owned by the Wertheimer family, who had invested in the cosmetics company Bourjois at the end of the nineteenth century. The Wertheimers took control of the entire Chanel business in the 1950s. Since then, haute couture and perfumery have been combined in one company.[24]

Secondly, the luxury perfumery sector includes a large number of companies specialized in this activity and the neighboring cosmetics sector. Most of them have their own branded products, such as Coty, L'Oréal, and Shiseido. They also manufacture fragrances under license for fashion brands owned by other companies. It is their ability to develop, produce and sell luxury fragrances that give these specialized companies their competitive advantage in this market. Among them, it is worth mentioning the presence of companies that do not own their own brands and that have specialized in licensed production, such as Interparfums and EuroItalia, both of which are in the Deloitte top 100. The case of Interparfums highlights the opportunity that the massive diversification of the fashion industry towards accessories since the 1990s represents for building a competitive business model.[25]

Interparfums was founded in France in 1982 by two young businessmen from the ESSEC business school, Philippe Benacin and Jean Madar. Their goal was to bring to the market inexpensive perfumes that mimicked luxury products. Three years later, they created Jean Philippe Fragrances Inc. in the United States, listed on the New York Stock Exchange and controlled by themselves (59.3 percent of the capital in 1996). It was a financial operation that allowed them to raise the capital needed to create and buy other companies. They founded Elite Parfums Ltd (1989) for the production and sale of premium perfumes, acquired several licenses for fashion brands, including Burberry

Image 6.3 Perfumes Chanel, Osaka, 2020.
Source: author.

(1993), and bought the Molyneux and Weil brands (1994).[26] The company was small at the time, with sales of less than $50 million in 1992. The runaway success of Burberry perfumes soon showed the potential for repositioning itself towards the production and sale of luxury goods. In 1999, sales rose to $87 million, 38 percent of which was generated by the British designer's products.

Benacin and Madar decided to abandon mass-market perfumery and imitations of famous products to focus on the luxury segment. The new expansion strategy for fashion brands was based on the expansion of accessories and offered extraordinary opportunities.[27] Jean Philippe Fragrances Inc. changed its name to Inter Parfums in 1999 and increased the number of licenses with luxury brands. The main ones are signed with Paul Smith (1998), Christian Lacroix (1999), Céline (2000), Lanvin (2004), Van Cleef & Arpels (2007), Jimmy Choo (2009), Montblanc (2010), Boucheron (2010), and Dunhill

(2012). The signing of two contracts with LVMH brands (Christian Lacroix and Céline) was a landmark event. It led to the arrival of Bernard Arnault's conglomerate in the capital of Inter Parfums for approximately 20 percent. Admittedly, this cooperation was of limited duration—LVMH sold Christian Lacroix in 2005, and the Céline license expired in 2007, after which the conglomerate withdrew from the capital. However, this temporary collaboration gave Interparfums legitimacy in the global luxury market and provided the opportunity to hire former LVMH managers, who are still employed today.

Nevertheless, Burberry was the main driver of Interparfums' extraordinary growth, with sales increasing from $101.6 million dollars in 2000 to a peak of 654.1 million in 2012. From 2003 to 2011, Burberry consistently accounted for more than half of its sales (Figure 6.3). Thus, when the British company announced, in 2012, its decision to end the license—sold in 2017 to Coty after a few years of internal management—the shock was significant for the Franco-American perfumer.[28] Turnover fell to $468.5 million in 2015. However, unlike the Japanese textile manufacturer Sanyo Shokai, which never managed to recover from the loss of its Burberry license in the apparel business,[29] Interparfums reacted by multiplying licenses for the United States or the whole world (Karl Lagerfeld, 2012; Shanghai Tang, 2013; Abercrombie & Fitch, 2014; Coach, 2015; Graaf, 2018; Guess, 2018) and by taking over the Rochas brand from the American group Procter & Gamble (2015). This re-composition of the brand portfolio made a new phase of rapid growth possible.

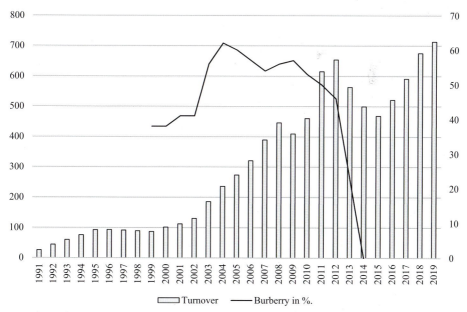

Figure 6.3 Interparfums Inc. sales, in millions of dollars, and Burberry's share, in %, 1991–2019.
Source: Interparfums Inc. *Annual Reports*, 1991–2019.
Note: The share of Burberry products is not mentioned before 1999.

6.4 Conclusion

The mastery of industrial production technologies thus gives a competitive advantage to many companies engaged in the luxury market. Contrary to the glamorous image of luxury goods made by hand by a craftsman, the strong presence of industrial groups among the world's leading luxury companies demonstrates the importance of the capacity to mass-produce quality goods. Companies as diverse as Volkswagen, Swatch, L'Oréal, or Luxottica are expressions of the industrial dimension of contemporary luxury. Of course, the business models are different. Some groups have a portfolio of diversified brands, acquired through takeovers, while others work essentially as suppliers of accessories. Luxottica and Inter Parfums depend mainly on external partners. This is also the case for the two American watch groups Fossil and Movado.[30] There are also intermediate models. L'Oréal or Swatch Group have, for example, developed cosmetics and watches under license, in parallel with their own products.

The presence of these industrial groups on the luxury market is not, however, their primary vocation. It is the result of a diversification strategy that responds to a new growth opportunity. The decade of the1990s marked a turning point. Volkswagen

Image 6.4 The development of perfumery is supported by firms from the chemical industry that develop new scents. The Swiss companies Givaudan and Firmenich are among the most important in the sector. Here, the Sensorium grand opening party, presented by retailer Sephora and Firmenich, in New York City, 2011.
Source: Getty Image, ID: 128372556
Credit: Cindy Ord / Stringer

relaunched Audi, Swatch Group bought Blancpain and made Omega a global luxury brand, L'Oréal decided to regroup its luxury brands within a specific division, and Interparfums signed its license with Burberry. The global expansion of the luxury industry at this time represented a tremendous opportunity for growth, an opportunity seized by many industrial groups.

The repositioning towards luxury, an area of high growth and profit potential, is accompanied by a risk related to the management of entry-level and mass brands, where competition can be fierce in the global market. It was probably this intense competition that led Interparfums to abandon its own brands. However, since the competitive advantage of industrial groups is based on their ability to mass-produce quality goods, the guarantee of a production volume that ensures the functioning and development of competitive industrial capabilities requires maintaining companies in the various market segments. This is what car manufacturers have understood by introducing common platforms for their brands, just as the Swatch Group in the watch industry has done with a similar strategy.

CHAPTER 7
BRANDS WITH DEEP REGIONAL ROOTS

When Bernard Arnault announced his decision to buy the American jeweler Tiffany for €14.7 billion in November 2019, one of the last major independent jewelery brands came under the control of the conglomerate dominating the luxury industry.[1] The two top independent brands today are Chopard and Graff. LVMH already owned Bulgari and Chaumet. The aim was to establish itself as the world's largest jewelry group in the face of Richemont. Tiffany's high turnover ($4.2 billion in 2017) allowed LVMH to greatly expand its presence on the world market. However, despite this acquisition, there was still one company with a larger market share: the Chinese jewelry manufacturer and trader Chow Tai Fook.

The name may not mean much to readers who are not connoisseurs of the jewelry industry or have not had the opportunity to walk through some of China's major cities. Chow Tai Fook cannot be considered a global luxury brand. Indeed, it is anchored in a particular area: the Chinese cultural sphere. The sheer size of this market with over a billion people explains why a brand that dominates jewelry consumption in China has established itself as the world's largest jewelry brand. It is not the brand's expansion into the global market (as in all the other cases analyzed so far in this book) but its presence in a fast-growing region that explains its success.

Chow Tai Fook is not the only company in Deloitte's top 100 to grow from a strong regional base. Other Chinese and Indian jewelers have a similar profile. This is also the case for Japanese cosmetics manufacturers whose products are very successful in East Asia but who have not been able to establish themselves as global brands. This chapter, therefore, presents some of the world's leading luxury companies whose growth springs from regional roots.

7.1 The world's largest jeweler: Chow Tai Fook Jewellery

Jewelry is an area of the luxury industry characterized by a low level of concentration. According to the consulting firm Euromonitor International, the ten largest companies in this sector accounted for only 12.8 percent of the global market in 2018.[2] Although the trend is slightly upwards, since this share was 9.4 percent in 2010, the concentration is still very far from a sector such as watchmaking, where the ten largest companies accounted for around 73.5 percent of the world market in 2017.[3] Thus, in 2018, Chow Tai Fook became the world's number one with only a 2.5 percent market share, ahead of Richemont (2 percent) and another Chinese company, Lao Feng Xiang (1.7 percent). This is due to the extremely high number of small independent jewelry companies around the world. Unlike luxury sectors such as fashion, cosmetics or watches, financial and technological investments are relatively low, encouraging many artisans to develop their businesses locally.

Therefore, European jewelry brands, whether exclusive luxury or premium, constitute only a minority share of the global jewelry market, which is dominated by a multitude of small companies operating on a regional or national scale. The large markets of China and India offer growth opportunities to many local companies, but the latter have difficulty growing in foreign markets.

Chow Tai Fook is a diversified group controlled by the Cheng family, a wealthy Hong Kong clan that has invested not only in jewelry but also in finance, property, hotel management, transport, communications, and energy. Yet, it is the sale of jewelry that forms the basis of this business group.[4] In 1929, Chow Chi-Yuen opened a gold jewelry shop in Guangdong, which moved to Macau two years later. After the Second World War, against the backdrop of the civil war and the advance of the Communist Party, the company relocated to Hong Kong. The business was developed by Cheng Yu-Tung, the founder's son-in-law, who took over the management of the family firm in 1956 and embarked on diversification of activities, seizing the opportunities offered by the tremendous development of the British colony in the 1960s and 1970s. The jewelry division was made autonomous in 1961 under a dedicated subsidiary, Chow Tai Fook Jewellery, which established itself as one of the city's leading jewelry distributors, gaining a monopoly on De Beers diamond imports in 1964. Cheng consolidated his company's reputation in the jewelry business by introducing 999.9 thousand pure gold products and, in 1990, adopting fixed prices in his shops. As the company publishes almost no historical data, its development during the last third of the twentieth century remains largely unknown. The few reports published in the business press, however, suggest growth was slow and mostly limited to Hong Kong and Macau. Chow Tai Fook adopted various initiatives to diversify its business, such as the launch of men's jewelry (1987) or the export of pearls (1995), without much success. The company remained relatively modest in size: its network of sales outlets comprised only twenty-two boutiques in 1995.[5]

China's gradual conversion to a market economy and opening up to foreign investors were key steps in Chow Tai Fook's development into the world's largest jewelry company. The Cheng family also invested in numerous real estate and infrastructure projects in mainland China, developing an important network of friendships and business relations among the country's elites. They opened their first jewelry shop in Beijing in 1998, and the distribution network quickly spread throughout the whole country.[6] In 2010, the company inaugurated its 1,000th outlet, followed by its 2,000th in 2014. By 2019, it had almost 3,000 outlets. Apart from China, Chow Tai Fook's presence is mainly limited to the Far East. Although it also distributes watches—its extensive network of boutiques having attracted the attention of Swiss watchmakers, particularly Rolex—the company depends on jewelry, which accounts for around 90 percent of its turnover. This tremendous expansion was made possible by family capital, as well as by the IPO of a small part of the capital in 2011. However, the Cheng family still has control over the company, owning more than 89 percent of the capital in 2019.

Figure 7.1 Chow Tai Fook goods, Hong Kong, 2017.
Source: Wikimedia Commons.
https://commons.wikimedia.org/wiki/File:HK_%E8%A7%80%E5%A1%98_Kwun_Tong_%E5%89%B5%E7
%B4%80%E4%B9%8B%E5%9F%8E_APM_mall_shop_%E5%91%A8%E5%A4%A7%E7%A6%8F_Chow_
Tai_Fook_window_display_gold_items_May_2017_IX1_02.jpg

Although Chow Tai Fook is known for its extensive distribution network in Hong Kong and throughout China, it is also a company that has verticalized its production. Its three factories in Shenzhen, Shunde, and Wuhan make possible both mass production of basic jewelry and the manufacture of customized goods through digital technologies. In 2019, 16 percent of the company's total workforce of more than 4,700 people was employed in production activities.[7] The jewelry manufactured in these factories is an affordable luxury product that uses precious materials (gold, silver, platinum, diamonds, and stones) with an excellent price-quality ratio. This is the secret of Chow Tai Fook's growth: it responds to the demand of the new Chinese middle classes in a context of social and cultural transformation—for example, the popularization of the Western-inspired romantic wedding. However, the Chow Tai Fook brand remains little known outside the Chinese world. Chinese culture greatly influences the design of its products, and it does not rely on a story highlighting the creative and glamorous aspects that built the global fine-jewelry brand. The state of the distribution network is a perfect illustration of this difficulty in breaking out of its original cultural space. In 2019, the company had 3,134 outlets worldwide, of which only three were not in the Far East. These are American shops, notably from the 2014 takeover of diamond retailer Hearts on Fire Co.[8] Chow Tai Fook also has eighty-two outlets in Hong Kong, twenty-two in Taiwan, nineteen in Macau, and twenty in various Asian countries.

Although not engaged in the global market, Chow Tai Fook grew strongly due to its position in the world's largest luxury market: China. The comparison with Tiffany is striking (Chart 7.1). The turnover of the Hong Kong jeweler was not known until 2009.

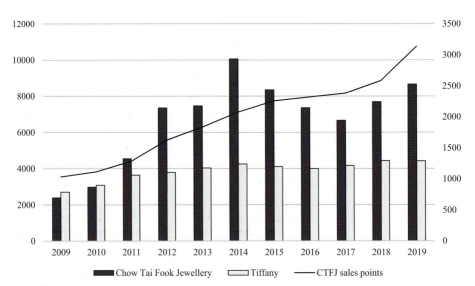

Chart 7.1 Chow Tai Fook Jewellery and Tiffany sales, in million dollars, and number of Chow Tai Fook Jewellery outlets, 2009–19.

Source: Chow Tai Fook Jewellery, *Annual Report*, 2011–2019 and Tiffany, *Annual Report*, 2010–2019.

Note: Chow Tai Fook Jewellery's turnover has been converted into US dollars based on HK$1 to US$0.13.

But at that time, as in 2010, it was close to Tiffany's, at between \$2.5 and \$3 billion. Yet since 2011, the two companies have followed fundamentally different trajectories. While Tiffany experienced a decade of very low growth between 2010 and 2019, Chow Tai Fook saw its revenue explode to over \$10 billion in 2014. However, this was an exceptional year. It was followed by a few years of decline that represented a normalization of business, then enjoyed a further increase after 2018. Chow Tai Fook's management does not give any other explanation for the decline in the years 2015 to 2017 than the vagaries of the Chinese economic situation (stock market panic of 2015–16). The impact of Hong Kong's anti-corruption policy and political conflicts on the company's management is not mentioned and is unlikely to have had any influence. However, the evolution of Chow Tai Fook's number of outlets, of which China consistently accounts for more than 92 percent, shows that no strategic change in the company has been envisaged since 2009. Online sales remain extremely low (4.5 percent of turnover in 2019). While the digitalization launched in the mid-2010s offered an additional experience to consumers, they continued to shop mostly in physical outlets.

7.2 From watches to jewelry: Titan Industries

India is also a country with many jewelry companies, a handful of which have made it into the world's top 100 largest luxury companies, four with sales of over \$1 billion in 2017. It is a large industry, employing around 2.5 million people in 2015, but fragmented, with small local companies accounting for about 80 percent of the overall market. Most of them are artisans who use traditional working methods. Their primitive organization means they lack the resources for the design and marketing of their products.[9] However, some companies have managed to adopt modern management methods and make jewelry a profitable and growing business. A case in point is Titan Industries, India's leading jewelry company.

Titan was originally a joint venture, co-founded in 1984 by the Tata conglomerate, one of India's most powerful business groups, and the state-owned Tamil Nadu Industrial Development Corporation (TIDCO). The aim was to establish itself as the country's leading watch company and to overtake the state-owned Hindustan Machine Tools (HMT), which started producing watches with Citizen's help in the 1960s but entered a phase of decline in the 1980s.[10] The first quartz wristwatches were launched in 1986, and the Titan brand was registered the following year. Production grew rapidly during the 1990s, and Titan became the leading Indian watchmaker. By 1993, it controlled 75 percent of the domestic market, thanks mainly to a distribution network of around 4,100 outlets. Attempts to expand into foreign markets, such as a stake in the American brand Timex (1992), participation in the Basel Watch Fair (1994), and the opening of a design office in Paris (1995), were not very successful. Between 1995 and 1998, Titan exported only 400,000 watches per year or around 10 percent of its total production.[11] The company's profitability also fell sharply during the 1990s (Chart 7.2). A solution had to be found to a situation marked by stagnating sales and declining profitability.

After several attempts at diversification (including the distribution of foreign watches, the acquisition of the Swiss watch brand Favre Leuba, and the launch of a perfume collection), jewelry enabled Titan to begin a strong growth dynamic. The company started a jewelry business in 1995, benefiting both from the Indian tradition of jewelry making and the relationships within the Tata group, which was active in the precious stones trade. The initial objective was to export jewelry to obtain the foreign currency needed to import watch products.[12] However, this new activity proved to be profitable in the domestic market, so the Titan management decided to strengthen its presence in this market. The idea was to thoroughly modernize the design and distribution of jewelry throughout the country. The standardization of products, the industrialization of production and the professionalization of sales through a nationwide network of mono-brand stores revolutionized the jewelry sector and prompted Titan to break its dependence on the unprofitable watch market. The watch business nevertheless allowed Titan to get to know and identify a target audience that also represented the heart of the jewelry business: young women. The company successively launched four brands aimed at specific targets (Zoya for traditional luxury, Tanishq for accessible luxury, Mia for young girls, and Caratlane for online sales), which had their own distribution network and benefited from modern marketing and advertising techniques. Tanishq is the mainstay of the Titan group's growth in jewelry, with mono-brand shops in thirty-five locations in 2000 and 178 in 2018. There is, therefore, a geographical expansion of the brand across the country. Titan is also exported, mainly to the Middle East, but foreign

Figure 7.2 Tanishq jewelry store, Mumbai, India, 2021.
Source: Getty Image, ID: 1236304854
Hindustan Times / Contributor

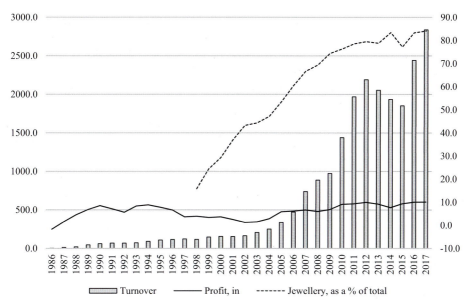

Chart 7.2 Titan Industries, turnover in million dollars, jewelry share in % and pre-tax profit rate in %, 1986–2017.
Source: Titan Industries, *Annual Reports*.
Note: Fiscal years end in March.

markets represent a very small share of its overall turnover (2.2 percent in 2010; 1 percent in 2018). These data show that it has remained a brand deeply rooted in the domestic market. Investment in building its brands and the continuous expansion of the distribution network are the basis for its strong growth.

The company's jewelry division generated profits for the first time in 2000, and its sales since 2005 have exceeded watch sales. The share of jewelry in Titan's turnover increased from 22.1 percent in 2000 to 53.4 percent in 2005 and 84.1 percent in 2017. At the same time, turnover grew almost exponentially from $155 million in 2000 to 2.8 billion in 2017, and the profit rate reached a record level since the company's foundation (over 10 percent in 2016 and 2017). Titan is a success story in India, just as Chow Tai Fook is in China.

7.3 Japanese cosmetics manufacturers

As for the beauty business, as Geoffrey Jones calls it,[13] it has such a cultural dimension that it is difficult, if not impossible, to have strong brands and products in all markets around the world. For example, although Japan became a major market for the European luxury industry in the 1970s and 1980s, perfumery has never been able to establish itself in this market because of a culture that emphasizes the absence of smell as an expression of cleanliness, purity and elegance. In 2019, Japan's share of LVMH's Perfumes and Cosmetics division was only 5 percent of revenue, compared to 12 percent for all divisions.[14] The cultural difference has not only an olfactory dimension but also an important visual aspect. The blonde, buxom Hollywood actress does not (any longer) embody the universal canons of beauty. These differences imply the need to develop different cosmetics for skincare and color intensity. They have led the giants of this industry to adopt a strategy of building brand portfolios through the acquisition of local companies (a multi-domestic strategy). This strategy is what allows L'Oréal and Estée Lauder to be present throughout the world. Cultural difference has also enabled companies with deep roots in specific regional contexts to experience limited internationalization. This is the case for Japanese cosmetics manufacturers.

The strong presence of Japanese companies among the world's largest luxury cosmetics and perfumery companies is an important feature of this sector. There are even three out of a total of twelve: Shiseido, Kosé, and Pola Orbis. This is the area in which Japanese companies are best represented, the other three in the Deloitte ranking being pearl manufacturer Mikimoto and two fashion groups, Onward and Sanyo Shokai. There is, therefore, a specificity of Japanese cosmetics companies that need to be analyzed to shed light on the foundations of this competitiveness.

The three Japanese luxury cosmetics manufacturers share a common characteristic. They are not global companies—that is, firms with a strong presence in Asia, Europe and the US—but multinationals whose internationalization is based on Asian markets. In 2015, Asia (including the domestic market) accounted for 65 percent of Shiseido's sales, 93 percent for Kosé and 88 percent for Pola.[15] This common specificity is certainly an expression of Japanese capitalism, marked by the difficulty of many Japanese companies to adopt global perspectives. But it is also necessary to take into account factors specific to the cosmetics industry. In East Asia, the idea of beauty is rooted in a cultural context particularly distinct from Western countries. The attention paid to the whiteness of the skin and the absence of body odor makes the Far East a tough market for Western companies to penetrate and one in which Japanese companies have a clear competitive advantage. They have used the regional cultural specificity to start their internationalization through neighboring markets. As an example, in 2018, Japan was the first exporter of cosmetics to China and the third to South Korea and Singapore (after France and the United States), while it ranked only eleventh for the whole world market.[16]

The largest of these firms is Shiseido, which, through its Prestige and Fragrance division, is the world's sixteenth-largest luxury goods company, with sales of $4.7 billion. Its origins date back to a Western-style pharmacy that opened in Tokyo's Ginza district in 1874 and which, from the late nineteenth century, imported and marketed foreign cosmetics. Owing to difficulties obtaining supplies from abroad during the First World War, it started producing cosmetics, enjoying great success during the interwar period thanks to its Art Deco-inspired advertising and packaging, which the son of the company's founder discovered in France in the 1920s. Shiseido, listed on the Tokyo Stock Exchange since 1927, also organized an extensive network of retailers throughout the country, which allowed the business to expand.

In 1949, after the Second World War, Shiseido restructured and re-listed on the Tokyo Stock Exchange. It began a timid international expansion in 1957 by establishing a sales

Figure 7.3 Advertisement for Shiseido soap, Japan, 1941.
Source: Wikimedia Commons
https://commons.wikimedia.org/wiki/File:Advertisement_for_Shiseido_Soap_in_1941.jpg

subsidiary in Taiwan, followed by exports to Singapore and production in Korea. However, the domestic market was the basis for growth—exports accounted for only 1 percent of total sales in 1970.[17] It enjoyed a position of uncontested leadership until the 1970s, after the successive appearance of foreign brands on the Japanese market, such as L'Oréal (1963), Estée Lauder (1967), and Avon (1968).[18] In return, Shiseido attempted to enter the American and European markets, where it sold its products by communicating traditional Japanese culture. It presented itself as a manufacturer of innovative, high-quality cosmetics (in the mid-1990s, it owned more than one hundred brands); however, these brands offered little intangible added value. They were much more like care products than luxury goods. In France, for example, Shiseido founded a joint venture with Laboratoires Pierre Fabre in 1986 to penetrate the French market. The focus was more on technical cooperation than on brand development, a positioning that limited expansion into foreign markets dominated by the glamorous brands of Western giants. In 1990, Shiseido founded Beauté Prestige International SA, a French subsidiary to develop licensed fragrances. It created fragrances for Issey Miyake (1992) and Jean Paul Gaultier (1993). However, this activity was thought of as a purely French business, and the group did not internalize the skills of this subsidiary. It was rather the intrinsic qualities of Shiseido products that led the company after the 1990s to reposition its internationalization towards Asian markets. It managed to compete with the big global brands on the Chinese market, thanks mainly to several joint ventures and local production with local partners.

At the beginning of the twenty-first century, however, Shiseido faced a declining domestic market in Japan owing to an aging population. Between 2006 and 2015, sales stagnated, and profitability declined. A new plan was adopted that year, marked by a strong desire to internationalize and move upmarket.[19] It was in this context that the company adopted a proactive strategy of positioning itself in the luxury market with the acquisition of foreign brands, such as Nars (2000) and Laura Mercier (2016) in the United States, and the signing of licensing agreements with others, such as Dolce & Gabbana (2016) and Tony Burch (2020). Nevertheless, half of its portfolio of prestige brands now includes cosmetics brands developed in-house and sold mainly to Asian customers.[20]

Kosé Corporation is the second-largest Japanese cosmetics manufacturer. Like Shiseido, the company does not specialize in luxury but is present in all market segments. It also bases its competitiveness on its ability to innovate and launch new skincare products. This focus on the intrinsic qualities of the product rather than on brand development explains its difficulty in establishing itself in the global market. Its internationalization has remained largely focused on Asia. In 2019, sales in Japan and the rest of Asia represented 72 percent and 15 percent of turnover, respectively.[21]

Kosé grew out of a small cosmetics manufacturing and sales company founded in 1946 by Kozaburo Kobayashi. The history of its development is not well known, as the family business discloses little information.[22] Kosé was a late entrant to the stock market in 1999 and remained under the control of the Kobayashi family, the main shareholder. As a general cosmetics manufacturer, Kosé soon became interested in the high-end segment,

Figure 7.4 Shiseido boutique in department store Daimaru, Osaka, 2020.
Source: author.

for which it created a special affiliate, Albion Co. (1956). It also collaborated with L'Oréal with whom it set up a joint venture in 1963. Expansion in Asia was rapid, with the company entering the Hong Kong (1968) and Singapore (1971) markets, followed by Taiwan, Thailand, and China in the 1980s. The share of these markets is not known.

However, it was mainly at the beginning of the twenty-first century that Kosé expanded into luxury goods. First, it signed a few licensing agreements, sometimes through its subsidiary Albion, with foreign companies such as Anna Sui (1998), Jill Stuart (2005), Rimmel (2006), Paul Stuart (2011), and the macaroon maker Ladurée (2012). Most of these are not major brands from the global fashion industry but brands that are well established in the Japanese market. Kosé's licensing strategy illustrates its national roots, which distinguishes it from Estée Lauder and L'Oréal.[23]

Subsequently, it acquired Phil International, Inc. (2002), a company that specialized in developing high-quality dermatological products, and Tarte, Inc. (2014), a small premium natural makeup company. Both companies are American, and their acquisition was an opportunity for Kosé to strengthen its presence outside Japan. Finally, the company multiplied its own brands, such as Beauté de Kosé (2001), Addiction for makeup (2009), and Awake, a former brand repositioned as vegetarian cosmetics (2017). This move upmarket, which focused on dermatological products, was accompanied by a strengthening of internationalization. Sales subsidiaries were opened in South Korea

(2001), Vietnam (2001), India (2013), Indonesia (2014), the USA (2015), and Brazil (2016). Expanding the business by entering new markets, increasing the number of products (only luxury and premium goods have been mentioned here) and acquiring companies led to a sharp increase in turnover from 94.5 billion yen in 1995 ($1 billion) to 332.9 billion in 2018 ($3 billion). This expansion also allowed the share of sales in Japan to fall below 80 percent and that of the Americas and Europe to reach 10 percent in 2017.

Finally, the third Japanese high-end cosmetics manufacturer, Pola Orbis Holdings, has a very similar trajectory to Shiseido and Kosé.[24] The main difference is that Pola has not been engaged in building a diversified brand portfolio. Its origins go back to a chemical company founded in Shizuoka in 1929, whose cosmetics division spun off to form Pola, Inc. In 1946, the company developed dermatological care products that it marketed in Japan under the Pola brand. In particular, it developed various products for maintaining skin whiteness, which corresponded to a demand from local female customers. In the 1980s, a second brand, Orbis, was introduced for high-quality oil-free cosmetics. Pola's success in the Japanese market, thanks to adopting a door-to-door sales consultancy system, meant that the company did not seek to expand outside Japan. Despite entering the Chinese (2004) and Taiwanese (2006) markets, its overseas sales amounted to less than 10 percent of its turnover in 2010.

A marked change in strategy occurred in 2010 with its listing on the Tokyo Stock Exchange. It used the capital raised to acquire companies with brands that allowed expansion outside Japan. The specificity of Pola and Orbis products made it difficult to enter Western markets. Pola Orbis Holdings, therefore, acquired H2O Plus Holdings in the US (2011) and Jurlique International in Australia (2012). However, these acquisitions only contributed slightly to the internationalization of the company. Sales increased from 165.2 billion yen in 2010 ($1.9 billion) to 248.6 billion in 2018 ($2.3 billion), but the share of foreign brands was only 10.7 percent in 2018.[25]

7.4 Conclusion

The Asian jewelry and cosmetics companies examined in this chapter are among the top luxury companies because they are well established in the world's largest markets, not because they have global brands. The specificities of these sectors enabled some companies to develop as regional players. Jewelry is a very low-concentration sector where local brands are evident. As for cosmetics, they are based on the commodification of a cultural value that is strongly anchored in regional areas: beauty. Therefore, it is the demographic and cultural characteristics of certain markets that make it possible for local companies to emerge alongside the major players in the global luxury sector.

Beyond this similarity, however, it is necessary to underline a profound difference between Asian jewelry manufacturers and Japanese cosmetics producers. For the former, the cultural barrier is weaker and provides less protection from luxury conglomerates. The big names in high jewelry, such as Bulgari, Cartier, and Tiffany, are well established in the Asian markets, where they dominate the exclusive luxury segment. This dominance is why companies like Chow Tai Fook and Titan focus on the accessible luxury segment, with products that appeal to a mass of customers rather than the new super-rich classes. They support the democratization of luxury goods consumption. The context is different for cosmetics and perfumery because the cultural barrier plays a protective role. Thus, companies like Shiseido have an extensive portfolio of products and brands to address specific customer targets, from entry-level to luxury. The mastery of production technologies and product development know-how is the basis of their competitive advantage, in the same way as the industrial groups presented in the previous chapter.

How can companies move beyond regional anchoring? Can Chinese and Indian jewelers, as well as Japanese cosmetics manufacturers, establish themselves as global players? Technical skills are not the issue, as all the firms studied in this chapter have mastered producing high-quality products. Here, too, the answer to the question differs according to the sector. Shiseido is clearly the company that has adopted the most active strategy for global expansion by acquiring foreign brands. The acquisition of companies in other parts of the world, as L'Oréal or Estée Lauder have been doing for several decades, allows for a portfolio of diversified brands anchored in particular cultural spaces and offering the company that owns them a presence in the main markets of the world. This strategy is also pursued, albeit more timidly, by other Japanese cosmetics companies. However, in the jewelry sector, no similar trend can be observed, despite the existence of many small, locally based companies around the world, all of which are targets for potential acquisition. In 2018, Euromonitor listed no fewer than twenty-eight jewelry brands with between 0.1 percent and 0.2 percent of the global market share, twenty-four of which did not belong to the conglomerates LVMH, Richemont and Kering.[26] Therefore, the lack of global ambition among Asian jewelers is more the result of a strategic choice than intrinsic difficulties in creating a portfolio of diversified brands.

CHAPTER 8
THE NEW LUXURY BRANDS

In 2017, after having associated her name with the development of accessories for several fashion houses, such as Armani, Dior and Gucci, the singer Rihanna (followed by tens of millions of people on social media networks) launched a cosmetics collection under the Fenty brand, which was already within LVMH.[1] Then, in 2019, she launched her own couture brand in collaboration with LVMH. This marked the first time Bernard Arnault's conglomerate had released a new luxury fashion brand since the launch of Christian Lacroix in 1987. Although the operation was not as successful as expected, owing in part to the COVID-19 crisis, which broke out shortly after its debut, and despite LVMH announcing the suspension of the couture activities of this brand in February 2021,[2] this attempt nonetheless illustrates that new brands continue to emerge within the global luxury industry.

Also, although only five of the world's top 100 luxury companies in 2017 were founded after 2000, this does not mean that luxury is not renewing itself. Numerous brands are launched every year across the globe, and conglomerates remain focused on renewing their brand portfolio. For example, of the seventy-six brands owned in 2019 by LVMH, ten were created in the twenty-first century.[3]

What are the business models behind these companies? How do they differ from older brands based on the exploitation of heritage? This chapter presents three main strategies used by the new luxury brands: reviving the "sleeping beauties," developing a casual luxury market, and technological innovation.

8.1 Revival of "sleeping beauties": Blancpain

The new marketing strategies based on heritage, which became a common practice in the luxury industry in the 1980s and 1990s,[4] led to the revival of several brands that had fallen into oblivion. Those that have strong specificities, such as the personality and talent of their founder (the watchmaker Abraham-Louis Breguet), the style of their products (the fashion house Elsa Schiaparelli), or the legend attached to their name (the Orient Express train), have a potential for growth thanks to the exploitation of a narrative that emphasizes the continuity of their reputation.[5] Not all "sleeping beauties" are destined for success, however. The revival of several French haute couture brands, such as Madeleine Vionnet and Paul Poiret, failed.[6] The same is true in the Swiss watch industry, where Swatch Group abandoned its Léon Hatot jewelry brand, acquired in 1999, and failed to make Jaquet Droz, acquired and relaunched in 2000, a dominant brand in the exclusive luxury segment. These examples demonstrate that the prestige of heritage is not enough to make it a profitable brand in the global luxury market. The current message of the brand, the products offered to the public and the image of its past must be part of a consistent heritage strategy. The revival of the Blancpain watch brand in the 1980s is an excellent illustration of these issues.

The Swiss watch industry was in trouble during the years 1975–85. The oil crisis and the sharp rise in the Swiss franc following the end of the Bretton Woods system highlighted the loss of competitiveness of Swiss watchmaking companies against their Japanese competitors, Seiko in particular. After the interwar period, Seiko adopted a strategic objective that enabled them to become the world leader in the first part of the 1980s: the mass production of high-precision watches. The switch to quartz strengthened the competitiveness of Japanese firms but was not the cause of it. The industrial reorganization of the Swiss watchmaking industry—carried out under the aegis of the consultant Nicolas G. Hayek and characterized by a series of mergers that gave rise in 1983 to the Société Suisse de Microélectronique et d'Horlogerie (SMH, renamed Swatch Group in 1998)—enabled the Swiss watchmaking industry to regain its competitiveness.[7] The rationalization undertaken by Hayek and the launch of the Swatch were the main driving forces.[8]

At the same time, Jean-Claude Biver, a young entrepreneur trained at Audemars Piguet and Omega, and Jacques Piguet, director of Frédéric Piguet SA, one of the few independent manufacturers of high-end mechanical watch movements, bought the Blancpain brand. Blancpain had evolved from Rayville SA–Montres Blancpain, a small family business acquired in 1961 by the Société Suisse pour l'industrie horlogère (SSIH). SSIH was the largest watchmaking group in Switzerland at the time and included the Omega and Tissot manufacturers.[9] This acquisition, aimed at increasing production capacity, enabled Omega to source small-caliber jewelry watches, one of Blancpain's specialties after the Second World War. However, the brand was gradually abandoned by SSIH, which became part of SMH in 1983. That was the same year that Biver and Piguet acquired the Blancpain brand. They founded Blancpain SA with a capital of 50,000 francs (about $24,000) and the support of Credit Suisse.[10] This gave them the capacity to produce excellent mechanical watches—thanks to movements supplied by Frédéric Piguet SA. With archive documents showing that the Blancpain family had been active in watchmaking since 1735, their brand could be considered the oldest in Switzerland. On this basis, they launched a new business model.

The strategy adopted by Biver, called by the Swiss press a "seller of nostalgia,"[11] went against the grain of the industry as a whole. Rejecting quartz, Biver built the image of a brand based on tradition and technical excellence, the foundations of the company's upmarket positioning. He set up the company in Le Brassus, a village in the Vallée de Joux, which is the historical headquarters for the production of highly complicated Swiss watches. This location in a region that represented watchmaking excellence and where such companies as Audemars Piguet and Jaeger LeCoultre had been present since their founding in the nineteenth century reinforced Blancpain's technical legitimacy. Moreover, in declaring the year 1735 as the year it began and in advertising its watches (often with many complications such as moon phases, tourbillon, erotic figures, etc.) as "made in the

SINCE 1735 THERE HAS NEVER BEEN A QUARTZ BLANCPAIN WATCH.
AND THERE NEVER WILL BE.

BLANCPAIN

Tourbillon

After the invention of the tourbillon in 1795, watchmakers succeeded in offsetting the effects of gravitation and hence providing mechanical watches with optimum precision.

Housed in a small mobile cage, the balance and escapement make one rotation per minute, the effect of which is to cancel out the rate variations.

Catalogue and video BLANCPAIN SA CH-1348 Le Brassus, Switzerland
Tel 0041-21 845 40 92 Fax 0041-21 845 41 88

Today, Blancpain has perfected and miniaturized this masterpiece of watch-making art and created the first tourbillon in the world with eight days power reserve.

This particularly sophisticated piece of horological engineering reflects the virtuosity and innovative spirit of Blancpain's enthusiastic team of master watchmakers, who view the tourbillon as a salute to the classic art of watchmaking they so ably perpetuate.

Figure 8.1 Advertisement for Blancpain in China, 1994.
Source: *Europa Star: China*, vol. 33, 1994, p. 7. © Archives Europa Star.

tradition of 18th century master watchmakers," Blancpain was proclaiming itself "the oldest watch brand in the world." The strategy worked as it enjoyed rapid success.[12] It organized a distribution system according to the principles of the luxury industry: sale through an exclusive network of specialized retailers throughout the world, limited production and high unit prices. The company's turnover rose sharply from 4.9 million francs in 1984 ($2.1 million) to around 60 million in 1991 ($41.8 million).[13] It was bought by SMH in 1992. Blancpain was a pure marketing project based on a precise idea (to offer mechanical watches embodying the tradition of Swiss watchmaking excellence) that led to formidable entrepreneurial success. Biver showed the way to luxury, and it was this know-how that SMH internalized in 1992. Moreover, after joining the group, Biver took charge of repositioning Omega in the accessible luxury segment, an operation once again crowned with success.[14]

8.2 The rise of casual luxury: Ralph Lauren

However, not all new luxury brands are the result of a heritage strategy. Identifying a niche in the luxury market brings the opportunity to launch a new brand to meet a new need. This was the case for New York fashion designers who developed independent labels for casual luxury clothing collections in the 1960s and 1970s to break away from the classic image of European brands. The growing relocation of the American textile industry to Latin America and Asia facilitated the launch of brands without owning a production system. American-style luxury is based on the identity of designers, and production is mostly subcontracted.

Ralph Lauren was the first of the New York fashion designers to establish himself as a representative of these new luxury brands. He founded his company in 1967. The following year, Calvin Klein set up his business. Their success in the 1970s led to a new generation of designers opening their firms in the 1980s, such as Tommy Hilfiger, Donna Karan (DKNY brand), and Michael Kors. The renewal continued in the following decades, with a positioning and business model that remained similar. These men and women were not fashion designers in the classic European sense of the term. They were entrepreneurs who developed strong brands based on their personalities and used them not only for clothing but also for a whole range of accessories. In a book published in 1999, Teri Agins, a journalist for the *Wall Street Journal*, took a hard look at these designers whose actions were determined by marketing and not artistic creation. She described Ralph Lauren and his rival Tommy Hilfiger as:

> designers without portfolios, neither had apprenticed in Paris, nor studied fashion in school or anywhere else. They didn't sketch; they didn't sew; they hardly designed, so to speak.[15]

The work of these designers in the fashion and luxury industry was disruptive. It demonstrated that building strong brands was possible on the margins of the heritage strategy followed by European companies. The luxury conglomerates were not insensible to this new business model. LVMH hired several of these designers as artistic directors of some of its brands, such as Michael Kors at Céline (1997–2004) or Marc Jacobs at Louis Vuitton (2001–13). As for Kering, it entrusted its Gucci and Yves Saint Laurent brands to Tom Ford—a Texan designer trained in New York—in the early 2000s. All these designers helped to diversify the French and Italian luxury brands into ready-to-wear and accessories. LVMH went further, acquiring stakes in the individual businesses of designers Marc Jacobs (1997) and Michael Kors (1999), as well as the Donna Karan brand (2001). However, the French luxury giant's interest in American designers was only temporary. LVMH divested its shares in Michael Kors' company in 2003 and sold Donna Karan in 2016.[16] As these brands were positioned more in premium fashion than in luxury, they did not correspond to the skills developed by LVMH.

If integration into luxury conglomerates is not the way for American fashion designers to grow, what is the business model for their development? Ralph Lauren Corporation, an independent, publicly traded company, is an excellent example of how New York designers organize their firms.

With a fortune estimated by *Forbes* in 2020 to be $5.7 billion, Ralph Lauren is now considered the wealthiest fashion designer in the world.[17] Born into a Jewish immigrant family in the Bronx, he is a self-made man who symbolizes the American dream. Moreover, he built his business on an idealized image of America that values individual success. The Ralph Lauren brand embodies the casual elegance of the white upper classes (the so-called WASPs), the lone cowboy of the Great Plains and the businessman of the East Coast metropolis. The consistency of this image, combined with using high-quality materials, has allowed Ralph Lauren to establish himself as the leading American fashion designer.

Born in 1939, Ralph Lauren got his start in fashion with the launch of a tie line under the Polo brand in 1967.[18] After gaining experience with Beau Brummell Ties Inc., he set up his own company that year under the name Ralph Lauren Corporation (RLC).[19] The following year, he introduced his first full menswear collection, and in 1970 opened his first shop in Bloomingdale's, New York. In 1972, he diversified into women's clothing and launched his Polo shirt, which soon became iconic. The brand expanded in the US market during the 1970s. International expansion began in the following decade with the opening of a shop in London (1981). The 1980s also saw the first product diversification. The Ralph Lauren Home collection was launched in 1983 with a series of furniture and accessories for the home, sold in a style that also expressed the nostalgic and timeless vision of the American phrase *Home, sweet home*.

However, RLC's expansion is based primarily on its role as a fashion brand in the American market. Ralph Lauren multiplied his lines and collections and established himself as a high-end generalist brand in the United States. In the fiscal year 1996, 71.5 percent of pre-tax company profits came from the domestic market.[20]

Growth in the US market was based primarily on product diversification and the internalization of retail sales. During the early part of the 1990s, the company launched new clothing lines to build on the reputation of the Ralph Lauren brand. A sports and fitness collection was introduced in 1992, followed by a series of denim and vintage products (1993) and an entry-level line of Lauren women's clothing (1996). As for the increasing internalization of retailing, this took the form of mono-brand stores. While distribution through department stores was important from the beginning of the firm, direct sales in boutiques became increasingly important in the early 1990s. In 1993, RLC formed a joint venture with Perkins Shearer Venture, a company active in the retailing of clothing on the American market. Perkins Shearer Venture took over the management of a network of shops for RLC products. The joint venture was fully taken over by RLC in 1997. Retail was key to ensuring the continued growth of the brand and increased profits for the company. In 1995, direct sales still only represented 29.5 percent of turnover. There was, therefore, plenty of room for improvement, but this required increased financial capacity. In 1997, RLC was listed on the New York Stock Exchange and opened its capital to investors while guaranteeing Ralph Lauren continued control of his company through the issue of preferred shares.

The IPO rose over 700 million dollars and funded the expansion of the sales network.[21] The company enjoyed very strong growth, with turnover rising from $846 million in 1995 to over 6 billion in 2020 (Chart 8.1). The increase was particularly rapid in the 2000s. The share of retail sales was predicted to reach more than 60 percent of turnover in 2020. The network of mono-brand shops owned by RLC grew from 229 in 2000 to 367 in 2010 and 456 in 2020. In addition, since 1999, Ralph Lauren restaurants have been opened near some of its major shops around the world. Online sales in fashion, launched in 2000, have grown significantly since 2010, but the company does not publish detailed figures.

Figure 8.2 Polo Ralph Lauren, 2013.
Source: Wikimedia Commons.
https://commons.wikimedia.org/wiki/File:SEXY_Ralph_Lauren._Mannequins.jpg

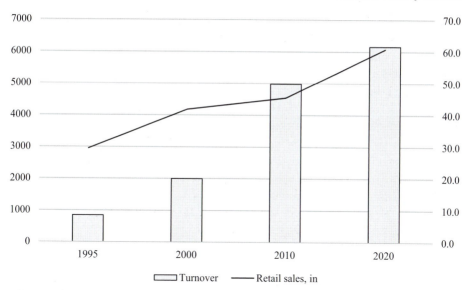

Chart 8.1 Sales of Ralph Lauren Corporation, in million dollars, 1995–2020.
Source: Ralph Lauren Corporation, *Annual Reports*, 1995–2020.
Notes: The years represent fiscal years that end in March. The 2020 fiscal year covers the period April 2019–March 2020 and is therefore only marginally affected by the COVID-19 crisis. Online sales are included in retail sales.

Diversification into luxury accessories accelerated in the mid-2000s. In 2006, RLC signed a licensing agreement with the Italian company Luxottica for the production of eyewear. Three years later, it created a joint venture with the conglomerate Richemont for the manufacture of watches. Based in Geneva, the company also launched a jewelry collection in 2010. RLC's desire to expand its reputation beyond fashion led it to recruit managers experienced with other brands. Until then, American entrepreneurs from fashion, department stores and finance had run the company. The appointment in 2014 of Valérie Hermann, former CEO of Saint Laurent Paris and manager of various brands at LVMH, as president of luxury collections perfectly expressed this ambition.[22]

However, despite RLC's tremendous expansion in the first two decades of the twenty-first century, this growth was largely based on the brand's traditional markets. In the fiscal year 2019, as yet unaffected by the COVID-19 crisis, sales in North America accounted for 50.8 percent of revenue, while Europe's share was 26.3 percent. Asia thus played a much less important role than European conglomerates and luxury brands.

Thus, the development of RLC was based on the exploitation of a single brand linked to the personality of the company's founder. There was no attempt to create a luxury group through the acquisition of other brands, which was probably due to the Lauren family's desire to maintain control of their business. The development model was, therefore, similar to that of Giorgio Armani SpA, with the difference that RLC did not verticalize the production of clothing. At the time of its IPO in 1997, the company did not have a production center. It subcontracted its manufacturing activities to about 180 companies around the world, mainly in Asia. Production in the US represented 42 percent of the total value of third-party orders. By 2020, the number of subcontractors had risen to over 500 and the share of US production had fallen to 2 percent, with China alone accounting for 25 percent of RLC production.[23]

American luxury fashion companies thus have a starkly different profile from European luxury companies. Firstly, they are not based on the exploitation of a historical tradition and heritage but on marketing projects aimed at building fashion brands for well-identified market segments. Designers such as Ralph Lauren or Tommy Hilfiger do not see fashion as a creative activity but as a purely commercial activity. They are entrepreneurs, most of them born and/or trained in New York City. Thus, a business model based on the relationship between haute couture (an investment in the brand through creative activities) and products intended for the general public (to make a profit) was foreign to American luxury fashion. In the United States, the brands, embodied by jet-setting designers, were self-sufficient. The absence of a narrative on creative gesture and craft tradition has made it possible to relocate production around the world without damaging the image of the brands.

Secondly, while the American fashion groups are certainly not absent from the Asian markets, they largely depend on the United States and Europe for their growth, except for Coach, the American company closest to classic European luxury. Their positioning on accessible and casual luxury puts them in a weak position in the face of the glamour of European luxury, whose power to attract seems limitless in the Far East.

So, the American fashion designer model has its limits. To improve the balance of its sales, Michael Kors Holdings (renamed Capri Holdings in 2019) acquired the British shoe and accessories manufacturer Jimmy Choo in 2017 and the Italian fashion designer Versace in 2018. Sales in Asia thus increased from only 4.6 percent in 2015 to 16.4 percent in 2019.[24] Dependence on the US market remained strong, but the acquisition of European brands suggested a more balanced growth.

8.3 Technological innovation as a source of luxury: Hublot and Richard Mille

Finally, several new luxury brands are built neither on the construction of a historical heritage nor on the exploitation of a brand associated with a famous designer but on technological innovation. Mentioning the examples of Lamborghini, Rolls Royce, and Ferrari, Jean-Noël Kapferer and Vincent Bastien explain that technology contributes to creating a world apart, beyond all constraints.[25] The luxury hotel industry has distinguished itself from its competitors since the nineteenth century not only by the excellence of the services offered to its customers but also by the creation of an innovative environment (lifts, electric lights, telephones, etc.).[26] In the automotive industry, the electric car manufacturer Tesla is also a direct result of new technologies.

Swiss watchmaking is again an excellent illustration for analyzing the role played by technological innovation in the formation and growth of luxury products. For the most part, it is a strategy of heritage and the enhancement of tradition that explains the repositioning of this industry towards luxury during the 1980s and 1990s, as shown by the example of Blancpain. However, the strong growth in Swiss watch exports since 2000 is not solely based on goods expressing the permanence of a tradition. Among the most successful brands of the last two decades, several are based on continuous innovation in material development and movement design.

Hublot is a case in point. This watch brand belongs to a Swiss company founded in 1980 that was one of the first to use rubber straps for its luxury gold and steel watches.[27] However, the company was small and loss-making in the early 2000s. In 2004, Jean-Claude Biver, the former boss of Blancpain and the man who relaunched Omega in the 1990s, invested in the company and took over the reins.[28] Inspired by the originality of the products launched by Hublot, he developed the concept of *fusion* and multiplied the number of watch models built with new materials, developed in-house or in collaboration with the École Polytechnique de Lausanne (EPFL). In particular, Hublot designed high-tech ceramics in various colors, scratch-resistant 18-carat gold, and synthetic sapphires.[29] These technological innovations enabled the brand to offer innovative products in the exclusive luxury segment, products that met with phenomenal success. Sponsorship of major events and famous footballers also contributed significantly to the brand's reputation. Hublot's turnover rose from around 29 million francs in 2004 ($23.3 million) to 150 million in 2007 ($125 million), leading LVMH to buy the company in 2008.[30] It continued to grow, reaching sales estimated at 640 million francs in 2019 ($646 million), making it the twelfth-largest watch brand in the world in terms of turnover.[31]

The trajectory followed by Hublot is far from unique. Its main rival is Richard Mille, which remains independent to this day. Founded in 1999 by a former sales executive of

Figure 8.3 Hublot Manufacture, Nyon, Switzerland, 2016.
Source: Wikimedia Commons.
https://commons.wikimedia.org/wiki/File:Hublot_Manufacture_Nyon_Passerelle.jpg?uselang=fr

the French watchmaking group Matra and a Swiss watch manufacturer, the company collaborates with a renowned manufacturer while developing innovative products. It launched its first watches in 2001. Audemars Piguet is involved in the development of this new brand through its subsidiary Renaud Papi. This enabled Richard Mille to internalize the most complex classic mechanical watchmaking skills, such as tourbillons.[32] But above all, the alliance between watchmaking tradition, new materials and a futuristic design gave the brand a positioning close to Hublot. On its website, it presents itself as a promoter of what it calls *hypertechnology*.[33] It developed new ultralight composite materials in collaboration with a company close to the EPFL, showcasing the lightness and resistance of its watches by creating special models for sports personalities, such as tennis player Rafael Nadal. Richard Mille's turnover was estimated at 98 million francs in 2010 ($94 million) and 900 million in 2019 ($910 million).[34]

The examples of Hublot and Richard Mille demonstrate that even in a sector that focuses its communication on the heritage of a centuries-old tradition, technological innovation can be the source of a luxury strategy. This does not mean, however, that technical innovation in itself ensures success in this field. The difficulties of brands such as Roger Dubuis (founded in 1995 and acquired by Richemont in 2008) or Ulysse Nardin (founded in 1846 and acquired by Kering in 2014) illustrate that the use of new materials and the development of innovative designs are not enough to create a luxury brand with strong growth potential. A core concept, like *fusion* for Hublot or *hypertechnology* for Richard Mille, makes it possible to develop products consistent with strong brand positioning.

Figure 8.4 Richard Mille tourbillon watch Alain Prost, 2018.
Source: Wikimedia Commons.
https://commons.wikimedia.org/wiki/File:RM_70-01_Tourbillon_Alain_Prost_(2).jpg

8.4 Conclusion

This chapter has presented three strategies that have launched new luxury brands since the end of the twentieth century. It is worth briefly discussing what they have in common and what makes them different.

All the brands analyzed above were born of marketing projects. The identification of a potential market for products with a strong message (the Swiss watchmaking tradition for Blancpain, American casual fashion for Ralph Lauren or the development of new materials with exceptional properties for Hublot and Richard Mille) is at the origin of the creation—or relaunch for Hublot—of these brands. This is a characteristic common to all these companies. Thus, it is not excellent know-how per se that makes a luxury brand possible, but rather, the desire to develop a brand (and particular products) leads to the mobilization of the necessary techniques and knowledge. Particular actors, such as the mechanical watch-movement manufacturer Piguet, the global clothing industry or the EPFL, support the technical realization of these projects. The global luxury market has become so competitive that new brands in this industry usually emerge in specific niches.

However, beyond this common characteristic, new luxury brands have distinct growth trajectories. The literature on the management of high-tech start-ups shows that they generally choose to go public or be acquired by another company to obtain the capital necessary for their development because organic growth is rare.[35] Most new luxury brands eventually become part of conglomerates or groups of companies—a similar trend to high-tech start-ups. Swatch Group and Hublot took over Blancpain and Hublot, respectively. In the American fashion industry, several designer-founded companies have also been integrated into groups. This is the case, for example, for Calvin Klein and Tommy Hilfiger, acquired by Phillips-Van Heusen (PVH) in 2003 and 2010. The path to independence followed so far by Ralph Lauren (listed on the stock exchange but maintaining family control) and Richard Mille (unlisted company) is, therefore, rare. The latter is similar to the Italian family business model discussed in Chapter 5 and faces the same challenges.

CONCLUSION

This book has shed light on how the modern luxury industry formed and developed. It has focused on the transformations of the 1980s and 1990s and the main types of companies that dominate this sector. To conclude, I would like to return to these organizational models, discuss their characteristics, and highlight the competitive advantages of luxury companies. Table 9.1 presents the specific features of the five models examined in this book. What can we learn from them?

First, the organization of these different firms is very similar. The capital comes largely from the financial markets (stock market listing), but its control remains in the hands of families, notably through the use of shares with preferential voting rights. The few companies with private capital are the independent family businesses (especially in Italian fashion) and the new luxury brands. However, the former often face serious financial difficulties that lead to their takeover by conglomerates, while the latter are usually start-ups that end up going public (like Ralph Lauren) or being integrated into groups (like Blancpain and Hublot). The financial markets, therefore, are an almost invisible but essential player in the modern luxury industry. The need to increase profits, which stems from being listed on the stock market, influences the management of companies, particularly in terms of global expansion, the democratization of products and the composition of the brand portfolio. While family control is a hallmark of the luxury industry, it is important to note that these are often not the same families that created and developed the brands decades or even centuries ago. Families like the Arnaults, Hayeks, Pinaults, and Ruperts are new families who have invested in creating groups and integrating brands. Their know-how comes from finance, logistics and administration, not from artisanal excellence or the mastery of traditional know-how.

Secondly, while all firms (apart from regionally based companies) are active worldwide, there are clear differences in the diversity of the brands. The conglomerates and industrial groups have many brands constituting a portfolio, but the conglomerates specialize in luxury goods, and the industrial groups are present in all markets. Owning a large number of brands allows economies of scale in production systems, logistics and distribution management. It also makes it possible to exploit industrial equipment—for example, the development of watches or perfumes for the other brands of the group (LVMH), as well as the signing of licenses for the manufacture of cosmetics (L'Oréal) or eyewear (Luxottica) for external clients. Independent family businesses and new companies generally specialize in operating a single brand or a small portfolio to maintain their autonomy. Companies with deep regional roots are in a similar situation: the difficulty of going international is often because of a marketing strategy characterized by a small number of brands. These various companies, therefore, do not have the advantages of conglomerates and industrial groups in terms of economies of scale.

Finally, production and distribution show close similarities between all these models of firms. All aim to verticalize the manufacture and sale of their products. The management of luxury brands requires direct control over these operations to guarantee the quality of the product and its distribution. Outsourcing is chosen in some cases because of the limited capital available. The relocation of production as a strategic objective to reduce manufacturing costs is exceptional and goes against the very philosophy of luxury, which aims to promote local production. It is only observed in a few specific cases, such as American fashion designers like Ralph Lauren.

This comparative analysis of the different organizational models in the luxury goods industry highlights the competitive advantages of conglomerates. Whatever the point of comparison, they are in a favorable position. This is no coincidence since it was precisely the entrepreneurs at the head of such groups who shaped the modern luxury industry in the 1980s and 1990s. Let us remember that this is a new industry. Most luxury brands have a long history, often beginning in the eighteenth and nineteenth centuries and enduring to the present day. This permanence through the centuries is what gives them the legitimacy to embody luxury today. However, the age of the brands is not the primary specificity of modern-day luxury. Large companies listed on the stock exchange now dominate this sector. Since the 1980s, these companies have adopted a new business model based on the exploitation of old brands and aimed at continuously increasing financial profits. The industry built on this managerial paradigm is new.

To conclude, it is worth saying a few words about the dominance of European brands and companies in the luxury industry. This dominance is due to the powerful attraction of an idealized European way of life, combining elegance, tradition, and hedonism. In the collective imagination of many countries, particularly in the Far East, this image of a European way of life expresses the outcome of an economic (rise in income and wealth), social (rise in individualism), and cultural (high level of education) development that broke with the values of traditional society. Europe's domination of the world was initially based on its economic, technological, and military power, which enabled the creation of empires. It was challenged in the twentieth century by the advent of the United States, decolonization, and the economic rise of the so-called emerging countries. In the context of a multipolar world in which Europe had largely lost its influence, the powerful attraction of European brands, a part of cultural imperialism, allows countries such as France, Italy, and Switzerland to maintain a presence throughout the world— their so-called *soft power*.

There are, of course, exceptions to this model of a European-dominated luxury industry. These have been discussed in detail in this book. However, they tend to occur in marginal sectors. Firstly, some brands are closer to a premium segment than to luxury per se—that is, embodied in quality products with a strong brand aimed at the mass market. This is notably so for American fashion and Asian jewelry. However, some of them can hardly be considered global. They have deep regional roots due to large domestic markets (Asian jewelry and American fashion) or cultural specificities

Figure 9.1 Virgil Abloh walks the runway during the Louis Vuitton Menswear Spring Summer 2020 show as part of Paris Fashion Week on June 20, 2019 in Paris, France.
Source: Getty Image, ID: 1157153084.
Credit: Pascal Le Segretain / Staff.

(Japanese cosmetics). Exceptions are American high jewelry (Harry Winston or Tiffany) and perfumery (Estée Lauder). They have developed around the glamorous image of New York and Hollywood stars, which has also contributed to the success of many Italian designers in their early days. Moreover, there is no fundamental contradiction with the image of Europe on the world market, insofar as these American brands convey individualistic and hedonistic values common to Western countries.

The domination of the global luxury market by Western brands has led in recent years to the emergence of crucial new challenges for companies, in the context of the growing influence of new generations of consumers. The increasing nationalist sentiment in China, as well as the rise of the woke movement and cancel culture in the US, show that the classic European lifestyle image attached to luxury brands is likely to turn into a weakness. As a result, major luxury companies have recently adopted various measures to affirm their support for ethnic and gender diversity, illustrating their dual desire to speak to new generations and to break away from cultural imperialism. The appointment of black American designer Virgil Abloh to head Louis Vuitton's menswear collection in 2018 is one of the best expressions of this new trend—but by no means the only one. This is undoubtedly a key issue if the European luxury industry is to continue its global market dominance in the decades to come.

Table 9.1 Competitive advantages of luxury companies

	Conglomerates	Independent family companies
Capital	Financial market	Private
Control	Family	Family
Number of brands	High	Low; single
Product diversity	High	Low
Global presence	Yes	Yes
Production	Verticalized	Verticalized; subcontracted
Distribution	Verticalized	Verticalized; subcontracted
Examples	LVMH, Richemont, Kering	Armani, Bulgari, Gucci, Zegna

Industrial groups	Companies with regional roots	New companies
Financial market	Financial market	Private; financial market
Family; shareholders	Family; shareholders	Individual; family
High	Medium	Low; single
Low	Low	Low
Yes	No	Yes
Verticalized	Verticalized	Verticalized; subcontracted
Verticalized	Verticalized	Verticalized
L'Oréal, Luxottica, Volkswagen, Swatch	Chow Tai Fook, Titan, Shiseido	Blancpain, Hublot, Ralph Lauren, Richard Mille

NOTES

Acknowledgements

1. See the bibliography at the end of the volume.

Introduction

1. Yves Messarovitch, *Bernard Arnault: La passion créative*, Paris: Plon, 2004, p. 9.

2. Danielle Allérès, *L'Empire du Luxe*, Paris: Belfond, 1992, Louis Bergeron, *Les industries de luxe en France*, Paris: Odile Jacob, 1998, Jacques Marseille, *Le luxe en France du siècle des lumières à nos jours*, Paris: Association pour le Développement de l'Histoire Économique, 1999, Jean Castarède, *Histoire du Luxe en France: Des Origines à nos Jours*, Paris: Éditions Eyrolles, 2011.

3. Werner Sombart, *Krieg und kapitalismus*, Leipzig: Duncker & Humblot, 1913 and Joseph Schumpeter, *Capitalism, socialism and democracy*, New York: Harper & Brothers, 1942.

4. Pierre-Yves Donzé, "Luxury as an industry," in Pierre-Yves Donzé, Joanne Roberts, and Véronique Pouillard, *Oxford Handbook of Luxury Business*, Oxford University Press, 2022, pp. 59–75.

5. Jean Noël Kapferer and Vincent Bastien, *The Luxury Strategy*, New York: Kogan Page, 2009.

6. *Ibid.*, p. 67.

7. https://stats.areppim.com/stats/links_billionairexlists.htm (accessed October 23, 2020).

8. https://www.forbes.fr/classements/fortunes/bernard-arnault-est-desormais-lhomme-le-plus-riche-du-monde/ (accessed May 31, 2021).

9. Interbrand, *Best Global Brands 2020*, https://www.interbrand.com/best-brands/ (accessed November 13, 2020).

10. Bram Bouwens, Pierre-Yves Donzé, and Takafumi Kurosawa (eds.), *Industries and Global Competition: a history of business beyond borders*, New York: Routledge, 2017.

11. Pierre-Yves Donzé and Rika Fujioka, "Luxury business," *Oxford Research Encyclopedia Business and Management*, 2017, https://doi.org/10.1093/acrefore/9780190224851.013.96 and Pierre-Yves Donzé, "Luxury as an industry."

12. Average exchange rates with the dollar are available at www.measuringworth.com

Chapter 1

1. See David Marx's blog, http://neomarxisme.com/wdmwordpress/?p=118 (accessed May 2, 2020).

2. Véronique Pouillard, *Paris to New York: the transatlantic fashion industry in the twentieth century*, Cambridge: Harvard University Press, 2021.

3. Mark S. Rosenbaum and Daniel S. Spears, "An exploration of spending behaviors among Japanese tourists," *Journal of Travel Research*, vol. 44, no. 4, 2006, pp. 467–73; Jose Luis Nueno and John A. Quelch, "The mass marketing of luxury," *Business Horizons*, vol. 41, no. 6, 1998, pp. 61–8.

4. Masahiro Yamada, "Parasite singles feed on family system," *Japan Quarterly*, vol. 48, no. 1, 2001, pp. 10–16.

5. Stéphanie Bonvicini, *Louis Vuitton: une saga française*, Paris: Fayard, 2004.

6. *Les Echos*, April 1, 2003.

7. Kyojiro Hata, *Louis Vuitton Japon: l'invention du luxe*, Paris: Assouline, 2004.

8. https://eu.louisvuitton.com/eng-e1/stores/japan (accessed October 20, 2019).

9. LVMH, *Annual Report*, 2002, p. 3.

10. Calculation based on data cited in Kyojiro Hata, *Louis Vuitton Japon,* 2004 and LVMH, *Annual Report*, 2002.

11. Rika Fujioka, Zhen Li, Yuta Kaneko, "The democratization of luxury and the expansion of the Japanese Market, 1960–2010," in Pierre-Yves Donzé and Rika Fujioka (eds.), *Global Luxury: Organizational Change and Emerging Markets Since the 1970s*, Singapore: Palgrave Macmillan. 2018, pp. 133–56.

12. Simon James Bytheway, *Investing Japan: foreign capital, monetary standards, and economic development, 1859–2011*, Cambridge: Harvard University Asia Center, 2014, pp. 217–20.

13. Tomoko Okawa, "Licensing practices at Maison Christian Dior," in Regina L. Blaszczyk (ed.), *Producing Fashion: Commerce, Culture, and Consumers*, Philadelphia: University of Pennsylvania Press, 2008, pp. 82–110; Akihiro Kinoshita, *Apapreru sangyo no maketingushi: burando kochiku to kouri kino no hosetsu*, Tokyo: Dobunkan, 2011.

14. Rika Fujioka, "Kodoseichoki ni okeru hyakkaten no kokyuka to tokusen burando no yakuwari," *Keizai ronso*, vol. 187, no. 3, 2013, pp. 95–110.

15. Rika Fujioka, *Hyakkaten no seisei katei*, Tokyo: Yuhikaku, 2006.

16. Akihiro Kinoshita, "Burando gainen no kakucho: 1970nendai Itokin no jirei," *Keizai ronso*, vol. 171, no. 3, 2003, p. 120.

17. Bytheway, *Investing Japan*.

18. Pierre-Yves Donzé, Ben Wubs, "Storytelling and the making of a global luxury fashion brand: Christian Dior," *International Journal of Fashion Studies*, vol. 6, no. 1, 2019, pp. 83–102.

19. Bytheway, *Investing Japan*.

20. Christian Dior SA, *Annual Report*, 2000 and https://www.dior.com/store/ja_jp?search=undefined&origin=pcd (accessed May 16, 2019).

21. Christopher M. Moore and Grete Birtwistle, "The Burberry business model: creating an international luxury fashion brand," *International Journal of Retail and Distribution Management,* vol. 32, no. 8, 2004, pp. 412–22.

22. Burberry, *Annual Report*, 2014–2015.

23. Tony Hines and Margaret Bruce, *Fashion Marketing*, Burlington: Butterworth-Heinemann, 2007.

24. Ying Wang, Shaojing Sun, Yiping Song, "Chinese luxury consumers: motivation, attitude and behavior," *Journal of Promotion Management*, vol. 17, no. 3, 2011, pp. 345–59.

Notes

25. Pierre-Yves Donzé, "How to enter the Chinese luxury market? The example of Swatch Group," in Donzé and Fujioka, *Global Luxury*, pp. 177–94.

26. Francesca Bonetti, "Italian luxury fashion brands in China: a retail perspective," *The International Review of Retail, Distribution and Consumer Research*, vol. 24, no. 4, 2014, pp. 453–77.

27. Thierry Theurillat and Pierre-Yves Donzé, "Retail networks and real estate: the case of Swiss luxury watches in China and Southeast Asia," *The International Review of Retail, Distribution and Consumer Research*, vol. 27, no. 2, 2017, pp. 10–11.

28. Bain & Co., *Eight Themes That Are Rewriting the Future of Luxury Goods*, 2020.

29. http://www.lcatterton.com/Press.html#!/LCAsia-Secoo (accessed November 22, 2020).

30. *Time*, October 26, 2018.

31. Swiss foreign trade statistics, communicated by the Federation of the Swiss Watch Industry.

32. *Ibid.*

33. Thorstein Veblen, *The Theory of the Leisure Class: an economic study of institutions*, New York: Macmillan, 1899; Georg Simmel, "Fashion," *International Quarterly*, vol. 10, 1904, pp. 130–55; Pierre Bourdieu, *La Distinction: Critique sociale du jugement*, Paris: Éditions de Minuit, 1979.

34. Okaw, "Licensing practices," p. 103.

35. https://www.lvmh.fr/les-maisons/vins-spiritueux/chandon/ (accessed November 26, 2020).

36. Christopher M. Moore and Grete Birtwistle, "The nature of parenting advantage in luxury fashion retailing: the case of Gucci Group NV," *International Journal of Retail & Distribution Management,* vol. 33, no. 4, 2005, pp. 256–70.

37. Kapferer and Bastien, *The Luxury Strategy*, p.179.

38. Danielle Allérès, "Spécificités et stratégies marketing des différents univers du luxe," *Revue française du marketing,* vol. 132, 1991, pp. 71–96. See also Donzé, "Luxury as an industry."

39. Thomas Piketty, *Le capital au XXIᵉ siècle*, Paris: Seuil, 2013.

40. *Ibid.*, p. 52.

41. Thomas Piketty, *Capital et idéologie*, Paris: Seuil, 2019.

42. Donzé, "Luxury as an industry."

43. John Armitage and Joanne Roberts (eds.), *Critical Luxury Studies: Defining a Field*, Edinburgh: Edinburgh University Press, 2016.

44. Pierre-Yves Donzé and Sotaro Katsumata, "High-end luxury wine demand and income inequality," *International Journal of Wine Business Research*, vol. 34, no. 1, 2022, pp. 112–32.

45. Comtrade database (https://comtrade.un.org/data/). These figures relate to French sparkling wines and not champagne alone, although the latter accounts for the overwhelming majority of exports by value.

46. OECD, https://www.oecd.org/industry/global-trade-in-fake-goods-worth-nearly-half-a-trillion-dollars-a-year.htm (accessed 25 April 2022).

47. Giacomo Gistri, "Consumers, counterfeiters, and luxury goods," in Pierre-Yves Donzé, Véronique Pouillard, and Joanne Roberts (eds.), *Oxford Handbook of Luxury Business*, Oxford University Press, 2022, pp. 524–44.

48. http://www.fhs.swiss/eng/stopthefakes.html (accessed April 25, 2022).

49. https://auraluxuryblockchain.com/ (accessed 25 April 2022).

50. *Harvard Business Review*, May 2019, https://hbr.org/2019/05/how-luxury-brands-can-beat-counterfeiters (accessed April 25, 2022).

51. Bain & Co., *Eight Themes*, p. 26.

52. Bain & Co., *Eight Themes*, p. 17.

53. Bain & Co., *From Surging Recovery to Elegant Advance: The Evolving Future of Luxury*, 2021, p. 14.

54. Peter Oakley, "Searching for pure gold: The impact of ethical gold sourcing certification programmes in the UK and Switzerland," *Environmental Science & Policy*, vol. 132, 2022, pp. 101–8.

55. *Le Monde*, May15, 2019.

56. Bain & Co., *Eight Themes*, p. 19.

57. The RealReal Inc., *Annual Report* (SEC filings, 10-K form), 2019–20.

58. Bain & Co., *Eight Themes*, p. 8.

59. *Le Figaro*, April 12, 2019.

60. *Le Monde*, September 2, 2008.

61. Lama Halwani, "The Online Experience of Luxury Consumers: Insight into Motives and Reservations," *International Journal of Business and Management* 15.11 (2020): 157–70.

Chapter 2

1. *Le Figaro*, November 28, 2006.

2. See Chapter 4.

3. JETRO, *Suisu no kinzoku-sei tokei bando: shijo chousa*, Tokyo: JETRO, 1980, pp. 1–9; Deloitte, *Global Power of Luxury Goods 2019*, Deloitte Touche Tohmatsu Ltd, 2019. (https://www2. deloitte.com/content/dam/Deloitte/ar/Documents/Consumer_and_Industrial_Products/ Global-Powers-of-Luxury-Goods-abril-2019.pdf).

4. Okawa, "Licensing practices," p. 103; Christian Dior SA, *Annual Report*, 2015–16. Since 2017, the Christian Dior brand has been consolidated in the LVMH group so that its turnover is no longer published.

5. "Giorgio Armani," *International Directory of Company Histories*, vol. 45, Farmington Hills: St. James Press, 2002, pp. 180–2; Reuters, January 14, 2017, https://www.reuters.com/article/ us-armani-results/giorgio-armani-2016-net-revenues-down-5-percent-2017-still-complicated-idUSKBN14Y0FP

6. *Le Comité Colbert en 2014*, Paris: Comité Colbert, 2014, p. 37.

7. Deloitte, *Global Power.*

8. LVMH, *Annual Report*, 2018, p. 16.

9. Geoffrey Jones, *Beauty Imagined: a history of the global beauty industry*, Oxford: Oxford University Press, 2010. See also Chapter 6.

10. *Le Figaro*, July 12, 2012.

11. *Time*, April 28, 2017.

12. https://www.apax.com/investments/consumer/ (accessed May 10, 2020).

13. See Chapter 7.

14. See Chapter 4.

15. Pierre-Yves Donzé and Shigehiro Nishimura (eds.), *Organizing Global Technology Flows: institutions, actors, and processes*, New York: Routledge, 2014.

16. See Chapter 3.

17. Véronique Pouillard, "Managing fashion creativity. The history of the Chambre Syndicale de la Couture Parisienne during the interwar period," *Investigaciones de Historia Económica-Economic History Research*, vol. 12, no. 2, 2016, pp. 76–89.

18. Pierre-Yves Donzé, "National labels and the competitiveness of European industries: the example of the 'Swiss Made' law since 1950," *European Review of History: Revue européenne d'histoire*, vol. 26, no. 5, 2019, pp. 855–70.

19. David M. Higgins, *Brands, Geographical Origin, and the Global Economy: a history from the nineteenth century to the present*, Cambridge: Cambridge University Press, 2018.

20. See Chapter 4.

21. See Chapter 3.

22. Pierre-Yves Donzé, "Fashion watches: The emergence of accessory makers as intermediaries in the fashion system," *International Journal of Fashion Studies*, vol. 4, no. 1, 2017, pp. 69–85; Diego Campagnolo, Arnaldo Camuffo, "Globalization and low-technology industries: the case of Italian eyewear," in Paul L. Robertson, and David Jacobson (eds.), *Knowledge Transfer and Technology Diffusion*, Cheltenham: Edward Elgar, 2011, pp. 138–61.

23. See Chapter 6.

Chapter 3

1. *Vontobel Luxury Goods Shop*, Zurich: Vontobel, 2018.

2. Hans Nadelhoffer, *Cartier*, San Francisco: Chronicle Books, 2007.

3. "Cartier Monde," *International Directory of Company Histories*, vol. 29. Farmington Hills: St. James Press, 1999, pp. 90–2.

4. Pierre-Yves Donzé, *L'invention du luxe: histoire de l'horlogerie à Genève de 1815 à nos jours*, Neuchâtel: Alphil, 2017, pp. 160–1.

5. Teresa da Silva Lopes, *Global Brands: The evolution of multinationals in alcoholic beverages*, Cambridge: Cambridge University Press, 2007.

6. U. Hakala, S. Lätti, and B. Sandberg, "Operationalising brand heritage and cultural heritage," *Journal of Product & Brand Management,* vol. 20, no. 6, 2011, pp. 447–56; Klaus-Peter Wiedmann, P. Hennigs, S. Schmidt, and T. Wuestefeld, "The importance of brand heritage as a key performance driver in marketing management," *Journal of Brand Management*, vol. 19, no. 3, 2011, pp. 182–94.

7. M. Urde, S.A. Greyser, and J. M. Balmer, "Corporate brands with a heritage," *Journal of Brand Management*, vol. 15, no. 1, 2007, p. 4.

8. J. R. Hall, "The time of history and the history of times," *History and Theory*, vol. 19, no. 2, 1980, pp. 113–31.

9. Henri-Irénée Marrou, *De la connaissance historique*, Paris: Seuil, 1954.

10. Eric Hobsbawm and T. Ranger (eds.), *The Invention of Tradition*, Cambridge: Cambridge University Press, 1983.

11. Kapferer and Bastien, *The Luxury Strategy*, p. 93.

12. Christian Salmon, *Storytelling: La machine à fabriquer des histoires et à formater les esprits*, Paris: La Découverte, 2007.

13. Claude Lévi-Strauss, *La pensée sauvage*, Paris: Plon, 1962; Bernard Crettaz, *La beauté du reste. Confessions d'un conservateur de musée sur la perfection et l'enfermement de la Suisse et des Alpes*, Carouge: Éditions Zoé, 1993.

14. Donzé and Wubs, "Storytelling and the making of a global luxury fashion brand: Christian Dior," pp. 83–102. Geoffrey Jones and Véronique Pouillard, "Christian Dior: a new look for haute couture," *HBS Case* 809–159, 2009.

15. http://interbrand.com/best-brands/best-global-brands/2017/ranking/ (accessed February 7, 2018).

16. See Chapter 4.

17. Christian Dior Couture, *Rapport annuel*, 1993, p. 8.

18. Christopher Moore, "The strategic value of the mono-brand store for European luxury fashion brands," in Pierre-Yves Donzé, Joanne Roberts, Véronique and Pouillard, *Oxford Handbook of Luxury Business*, Oxford & New York: Oxford University Press, 2022, pp. 353–77.

19. Christian Dior Couture, *Rapport annuel*, 1994, p. 13.

20. Okawa, "Licensing practices."

21. Christian Dior Couture, *Rapport annuel, 1993*, p. 3.

22. Christian Dior Couture, *Rapport annuel*, 2003, p. 15.

23. *Le Temps*, September 14, 2001.

24. Christian Dior Couture, *Rapport annuel*, 1996, p. 13.

25. Christian Dior Couture, *Rapport annuel*, 1994, p. 3.

26. Ginger Gregg Duggan, "The greatest show on earth: A look at contemporary fashion shows and their relationship to performance art," *Fashion Theory*, vol. 5, no. 3, 2001, pp. 243–70.

27. Christian Dior Couture, *Rapport annuel*, 2000, p. 4.

28. *Les Echos*, May 18, 2000.

29. *The Guardian*, September 8, 2011.

30. Christian Dior Couture, *Rapport annuel*, 2001, p. 4.

31. Karina Pronitcheva, "Luxury brands and public museums: From anniversary exhibitions to co-branding," in Donzé and Fujioka, *Global Luxury*, pp. 219–37.

32. Christian Dior Couture, *Rapport annuel*, 2006, pp. 2–3.

33. Françoise Giroud, et al., *Dior: Christian Dior, 1905–1957*, Paris: Éditions du Regard, 1987, unpaginated.

34. Jones and Pouillard, "Christian Dior."

35. Valerie Steele, *Paris Fashion: a cultural history*, London: Bloomsbury Publishing, 1998.

36. V. Mendes and A. de la Haye, *Fashion Since 1900*, London: Thames & Hudson, 2010.

37. Okawa, "Licensing practices."

38. Pierre-Yves Donzé and Ben Wubs, "LVMH: storytelling and organizing creativity in luxury and fashion," in Regina Lee Blaszczyk, Véronique Pouillard (eds.), *European Fashion: the creation of a global industry*, Manchester: Manchester University Press, 2018, pp. 63–85.

39. *Les Echos*, May 4, 1992.

40. https://www.dior.com/couture/fr_fr/la-maison-dior/depuis-1947 (accessed May 25, 2020).

41. https://www.dior.com/couture/fr_fr/la-maison-dior/dior-en-histoires/la-revolution-du-new-look (accessed May 25, 2020).

42. *New York Times*, November 8, 2010.

43. J.-L. Dufresnes, "La maison Dior et le monde, 1946–2006," in *Christian Dior et le monde*, Paris: Artlys, 2006, pp. 5–9.

Chapter 4

1. Alain Chatriot, "La construction récente des groupes de luxe français: mythes, discours et pratiques," *Entreprises et histoire*, no. 1, 2007, pp. 143–156; Hubert Bonin, "Reassessment of the business history of the French luxury sector: the emergence of a new business model and a renewed corporate image (from the 1970s)," in Luciano Segret, et al. (eds.), *European Business and Brand Building*, Brussels: PIE Peter Lang, 2012, pp. 113–35.

2. Patrick Eveno, "La construction d'un groupe international, LVMH," in Jacques Marseille (ed.), *Le luxe en France, du siècle des Lumières à nos jours*, Paris: Association pour le développement de l'histoire économique, 1999, pp. 291–321; Bonin, "Reassessment of the business history"; Donzé and Wubs, "LVMH"; LVMH, *Annual Reports*.

3. Louis Vuitton SA, *Annual Reports*, 1981–5.

4. Da Silva Lopes, *Global Brands*.

5. Eurostaf Dafsa, *LVMH*, 1987.

6. Bonin, "A Reassessment of the business history"; Andrea Colli and Michelangelo Vasta, "Large and entangled: Italian business groups in the long run," *Business History*, vol. 57, no. 1, 2015, pp. 64–96.

7. *Le Monde*, May 18, 2013.

8. *Financial Times*, April 26, 2017.

9. Nadelhoffer, *Cartier*.

10. *Feuille officielle suisse du commerce*, August 25, 1988.

11. "Vendôme Luxury Group," *International Directory of Company Histories*, vol. 27, Farmington Hills: St. James Press, 1999, pp. 487–9.

12. Donzé, *L'invention du luxe*.

13. *Time*, October 26, 2018.

14. Pierre Daix, *François Pinault: essai biographique*, Paris: Éditions de Fallois, 1998.

15. *Les Echos*, June 10, 1996.

16. http://www.groupeartemis.com (accessed July 25, 2016).

17. Moore and Birtwistle, "The nature of parenting advantage," p. 257.

18. Gucci Group NV, *International Directory of Company Histories*, vol. 15, Farmington Hills: St. James Press, 1996, pp. 198–200.

19. Barbara Smit, *Pitch Invasion: Adidas, Puma and the making of modern sport*, London: Penguin UK, 2007.

20. Alfred D. Chandler, *Scale and Scope: the dynamics of industrial capitalism*, Boston: Harvard University Press, 1990.

21. See Chapter 1.

22. Moore and Birtwistle, "The nature of parenting advantage."

23. Okawa, "Licensing practices," p. 103.

24. LVMH, *Letter to shareholders*, February 1994.

25. Lucien F. Trueb, *The World of Watches: history, industry, technology*, New York: Ebner Publishing, 2005, p. 285.

26. *Le Figaro*, May 2, 2012.

27. Pierre-Yves Donzé, *Histoire du Swatch Group*, Neuchâtel: Alphil, 2012, pp. 123–6.

28. Donzé, *L'invention du luxe*, pp. 175–7.

29. Messarovitch, *La passion créative*, p. 80.

Chapter 5

1. François-Marie Grau, *La haute couture*, Paris: PUF, 2000, p. 24.

2. See Chapter 3.

3. John Potvin, *Giorgio Armani: empire of the senses*, London & New York: Routledge, 2013.

4. Potvin, *Giorgio Armani*; Elisabett Merlo, "Italian fashion business: achievements and challenges (1970s–2000s)," *Business History*, vol. 53, no. 3, 2011, pp. 344–62.

5. Elisabetta Merlo and Francesca Polese, "Turning fashion into business: the emergence of Milan as an international fashion hub," *Business History Review*, vol. 80, no. 3, 2006, pp. 443–4.

6. Potvin, *Giorgio Armani*, p. 44.

7. *Ibid.*, pp. 82–96.

8. *Ibid.*, p. 89.

9. Merlo, "Italian fashion business," p. 352.

10. *Ibid.*, p. 353.

11. Potvin, *Giorgio Armani*, p. 105.

12. Merlon, "Italian fashion business," p. 353; *The Armani Group and Sustainability*, 2018 (annual report).

13. Merlo, "Italian fashion business," p. 349.

14. *Ibid.*, p. 351.

15. Elisabetta Merlo and Mario Perugini, "Making Italian fashion global: brand building and management at Gruppo Finanziario Tessile (1950s–1990s)," *Business History*, vol. 62, no. 1, 2020, p. 58.

16. Maria Carmela Ostillio and Sarah Ghaddar, "Tod's: a global multi-brand company with a taste of tradition," in Byoungho Jin and Elena Cedrola (eds.), *Fashion Brand Internationalization: opportunities and challenges*, New York: Palgrave Pivot, 2016, pp. 101–23.

17. Elisabetta Merlo, "Italian luxury goods industry on the move: SMEs and global value chains," in Donzé and Fujioka, *Global Luxury*, pp. 39–63.

18. Piergiorgio Re, et al., "The role of the founder's DNA throughout crisis: the revitalization of Moncler," in Fabrizio Mosca, et al. (eds.), *Global Marketing Strategies for the Promotion of Luxury Goods*, Hershey: IGI Global, 2016, pp. 266–83.

19. Elena Cedrola and Ksenia Silchenko, "Ermenegildo Zegna: when family values guide global expansion in the luxury industry," in Jin and Cedrola, *Fashion Brand Internationalization*, pp. 31–64.

20. "Ermenegildo Zegna," *International Directory of Company Histories*, vol. 63, Farmington Hills: St. James Press, 2004, pp. 149–51.

21. Cedrola and Silchenko, "Ermenegildo Zegna."

22. Elisabetta Savelli, "Role of brand management of the luxury fashion brand in the global economic crisis: a case study of Aeffe group," *Journal of Global Fashion Marketing*, vol. 2, no. 3, 2011, pp. 170–9; https://aeffe.com/group-profile/ (accessed June 20, 2020).

23. Andrea Colli and Elisabetta Merlo, "Family business and luxury business in Italy (1950–2000)," *Entreprises et histoire*, vol. 1, 2007, pp. 113–24.

24. "Gucci Group," *International Directory of Company Histories*, vol. 50, Farmington Hills: St. James Press, 2003, pp. 213–215; Moore and Birtwistle, "The nature of parenting advantage."

25. Moore and Birtwistle, "The nature of parenting advantage," p. 261.

26. Jose Luis Nueno and John A. Quelch, "The mass marketing of luxury," *Business Horizons*, vol. 41, no. 6, 1998, pp. 61–1.

27. See Chapter 3.

28. Gucci Group, *International Directory of Company Histories*, vol. 50, Farmington Hills: St. James Press, 2003, pp. 213–15.

29. See Chapter 4.

30. "Bulgari SpA," *International Directory of Company Histories*, vol. 20, Farmington Hills: St. James Press, 1998, pp. 94–7.

31. *Feuille officielle suisse du commerce*, December 16, 1975.

32. Donzé, *L'invention du luxe*.

33. "Bulgari SpA," *International Directory of Company Histories*, vol. 20, Farmington Hills: St. James Press, 1998, pp. 94–7.

34. *Journal de Genève*, September 24, 1990.

35. *Les Echos*, April 17, 2001.

36. *Les Echos*, August 3, 1998 and February 14, 2001; Donzé, *L'invention du luxe*.

37. *Les Echos*, June 14, 2004 and March 7, 2011.

38. Jean-Noël Kapferer, *Kapferer on Luxury: how luxury brands can grow yet remain rare*, New York: Kogan Page Publishers, 2015.

39. Euromonitor International, https://go.euromonitor.com/passport.html (accessed August 30, 2020).

40. Andrea Colli, *Edizione: the story of the Benetton Holding Company, 1986–present*, London: Third Millennium Publishing, 2017.

41. Elisabetta Merlo, "Italian luxury goods industry on the move: SMEs and global value chains," in Donzé and Fujioka, *Global Luxury*, pp. 60–1.

42. Kapferer, *Kapferer on Luxury*; *Les Echos*, September 25, 2018.

43. Andrea Colli, Alberto Rinaldi, and Michelangelo Vasta, "The only way to grow? Italian Business groups in historical perspective," *Business History*, vol. 58, no. 1, 2016, pp. 30–48.

Chapter 6

1. Audi AG, *A History of Progress: chronicle of the Audi AG*, Cambridge: Bentley Publishers, 1998.

2. Audi AG, *Geschäftsbericht*, 1985–2019.

3. Ludger Pries, "Accelerating from a multinational to a transnational carmaker: the Volkswagen consortium in the 1990s," in Michel Freyssenet, Koichi Shimizu, and Giuseppe Volpato (eds.), *Globalization or Regionalization of the European Car Industry?* Basingstoke: Palgrave Macmillan, 2003, pp. 51–72.

4. Paul Nieuwenhuis and Peter Wells (eds.), *The Global Automotive Industry*, Singapore: John Wiley & Sons, 2015.

5. Mary Quek, "Comparative historical analysis of four UK hotel companies, 1979–2004," *International Journal of Contemporary Hospitality Management*, vol. 23, no. 2, 2011, pp. 147–73.

6. Pierre-Yves Donzé, *A Business History of the Swatch Group: the rebirth of Swiss watchmaking and the globalization of the luxury industry*, Basingstoke: Palgrave Macmillan, 2014.

7. L'Oréal, *Annual Report*, 2019.

8. Jacques Marseille, *L'Oréal, 1909–2009*; Jones, *Beauty Imagined*.

9. L'Oréal, *Annual Report*, 2019; Jones, *Beauty Imagined*, p. 177.

10. Jones, *Beauty Imagined*, p. 371.

11. "L'Oréal SA," *International Directory of Company Histories*, vol. 8, Farmington Hills: St. James Press, 1994, pp. 129–31.

12. Jones, *Beauty Imagined*, p. 160.

13. *Ibid.*, pp. 204–5 and 324.

14. *Ibid.*, p. 207.

15. See section 6.3.

16. *Les Echos*, November 27, 2000; *Financial Times*, February 29, 2016.

17. L'Oréal, *Annual Report*, 2000.

18. *Les Echos*, April 7, 2009.

19. Campagnolo and Camuffo, "Globalization and low-technology industries"; Luxottica, *Annual Reports*.

20. "Luxottica," *International Directory of Company Histories*, vol. 52, Farmington Hills: St. James Press, 2003, pp. 227–30.

21. Eugénie Briot, *La Fabrique des parfums: naissance d'une industrie de luxe*, Paris: Vendémiaire, 2015.

22. Eugénie Briot, "1921: parfumer le monde," in Patrick Boucheron (ed.), *Histoire mondiale de la France*, Paris: Seuil, 2018, pp. 800–5.

23. Euromonitor International, https://go.euromonitor.com/passport.html (accessed August 30, 2020).

24. "Chanel SA," *International Directory of Company Histories*, vol. 49, Farmington Hills: St. James Press, 2003, pp. 83–6.

25. "Interparfums," *International Directory of Company Histories*, vol. 35, Farmington Hills: St. James Press, 2001, pp. 235–7.

26. *Les Echos*, January 25, 1994.

27. See Chapter 3.

28. *Les Echos*, April 3, 2017.

29. See Chapter 1.

30. For the case of Fossil, see Pierre-Yves Donzé, "Fashion watches: the emergence of accessory makers as intermediaries in the fashion system," *International Journal of Fashion Studies*, vol. 4, no. 1, 2017, pp. 69–85.

Chapter 7

1. *Le Monde*, November 25, 2019.

2. Euromonitor International, https://go.euromonitor.com/passport.html (accessed August 30, 2020).

3. *Vontobel Luxury Goods Shop*, Zurich: Vontobel Equity Research, 2018, p. 19.

4. Chow Tai Fook Jewellery, *Annual Reports*, 2011–2019 and https://www.ctfjewellerygroup.com/en/group/history.html (accessed September 25, 2020).

5. *Jewellery News Asia*, June 1, 1998 and October 1, 1998.

6. *South China Morning Post*, December 6, 2011.

7. Chow Tai Fook, *Annual Report*, 2020, p. 37.

8. *The Wall Street Journal*, June 18, 2014.

9. S. Madhavi and T. Rama Devi, "Problems of Indian jewellery industry," *International Journal of Management Research and Reviews*, vol. 5, no. 8, 2015, pp. 623–8.

10. Utpal Chattopadhyay and Pragya Bhawsar, "Effects of changing business environment on organization performance: the case of HMT Watches Ltd," *South Asian Journal of Business and Management Cases*, vol. 6, no. 1, 2017, pp. 36–46; Donzé, *Des nations, des firmes*, pp. 143–5.

11. Titan Industries, *Annual Reports*, 1987–98.

12. Titan Industries, *Annual Report*, 2000–1, p. 17.

13. Jones, *Beauty Business*.

14. LVMH, *Annual Report*, 2019.

15. Maki Umemura and Stephanie Slater, "Reaching for global in the Japanese cosmetics industry, 1951 to 2015: the case of Shiseido," *Business History*, vol. 59, no. 6, 2017, pp. 877–903, 878.

16. COMTRADE, HS code 33, 2018, https://comtrade.un.org/data/ (accessed August 21, 2020).

17. Umemura and Slater, "Reaching for global," p. 890.

18. *Ibid.*, p. 884.

19. Shiseido, *Annual Report*, 2015.

20. https://corp.shiseido.com/en/brands/ (accessed August 21, 2020).

21. Kosé, *Annual Report*, 2019.

22. Unless otherwise stated, the information in this section is taken from the brand's annual reports and website (https://www.kose.co.jp/), as well as the *Nikkei Shimbun* business daily, https://www.nikkei.com/ (accessed August 2020).

23. A similar phenomenon can be observed in the watch industry, where the Japanese groups Seiko and Citizen produce watches under licence mainly for fashion brands with a strong domestic presence. Pierre-Yves Donzé, David Borel, "Technological Innovation and Brand Management: The Japanese Watch Industry since the 1990s," *Journal of Asia-Pacific Business*, vol. 20, no. 2, 2019, pp. 120.

24. Eien No Bi Wo Motomete-POLA Monogatari, Tokyo: Pola, 1980.

25. Pola Orbis Holdings, *Annual Report*, 2018.

26. Euromonitor International, https://go.euromonitor.com/passport.html (accessed August 30, 2020).

Chapter 8

1. LVMH, *Annual Report*, 2019.

2. *Les Echos*, February 10, 2021.

3. LVMH, *Annual Report*, 2019, p. 15.

4. See Chapter 3.

5. Delphine Dion, "How to manage heritage brands: the case of sleeping beauties revival," in Donzé, Roberts, and Pouillard (eds.), *The Oxford Handbook of Luxury Business*, pp. 273–86.

6. Johanna Zanon, "Reawakening the 'sleeping beauties' of haute couture: the case of Guy and Arnaud de Lummen," in Blaszczyk and Pouillard (eds.), *European Fashion*, pp. 86–115.

7. Pierre-Yves Donzé, "Global competition and technological innovation: a new interpretation of the watch crisis, 1970s–1980s," in Thomas David, Jon Mathieu, Janick Marina Schaufelbuehl, and Tobias Straumann (eds.), *Crises–Causes, Interpretations and Consequences*, Zurich: Chronos, 2012, pp. 275–89.

8. Donzé, *A Business History of the Swatch Group.*

9. Marco Richon, *Omega Saga*, Biel: Fondation Brandt, 1998.

10. *Journal de Genève*, June 12, 1987.

11. *The New Daily*, October 13, 1991.

12. *Journal de Genève*, June 12, 1987.

13. *Journal de Genève*, June 12, 1987 and July 9, 1992.

14. Donzé, *A Business History of the Swatch Group.*

15. Teri Agins, *The End of Fashion: how marketing changed the clothing business for ever*, New York: Morrow, 1999, p. 83.

16. LVMH, *Annual Reports*; Kering, *Annual Reports*.

17. https://www.forbes.com/billionaires/ (accessed June 30, 2020).

18. *The New York Times*, September 29, 2015.

19. Ralph Lauren Corporation, *Annual Reports*, 1995–2020; company history on the brand's website, https://www.ralphlauren.com/rl-50-timeline-feat?ab=en_US_RL50_About_Slot_CN_S1_L1 (accessed July 2, 2020).

20. Ralph Lauren Corporation, *Annual Report*, 1998, p. 59. Figures not published before 1996. Turnover by region is not available for the second half of the 1990s.

21. *The Washington Post*, June 13, 1997.

Notes

22. She left her post in 2019, and it has not been filled.

23. CDN, *Annual Reports*, 1997 and 2020.

24. Michael Kors Holdings/Capri Holdings, *Annual Reports*, 2016 and 2020.

25. Kapferer Jean Noël, Bastien Vincent, *The Luxury Strategy*, p. 57.

26. Molly W. Berger, *Hotel Dreams: luxury, technology, and urban ambition in America, 1829–1929*, Baltimore: Johns Hopkins University Press, 2011.

27. *Le Temps*, April 25, 2008.

28. Pierre-Yves Donzé, "Industrial leadership and the long-lasting competitiveness of the Swiss watch industry," in Martin Guttmann (ed.), *Historians on Leadership and Strategy: case studies from antiquity to modernity*, Cham: Springer, 2020, pp. 171–91.

29. https://www.hublot.com/fr-is/craftsmanship/innovative-materials (accessed on May 25, 2021).

30. *Le Temps*, April 25, 2008.

31. Edouard Aubin and Elena Mariani, *Swiss Watches: polarisation accelerates further*, Morgan Stanley & Co., 2020.

32. *Europa Star*, vol. 24, 2003, p. 3. A tourbillon is a device that eliminates errors of rate in the vertical positions. It consists of a mobile cage carrying all the parts of the escapement, with the balance in the centre. It is one of the most complex mechanisms in mechanical watchmaking. It expresses the excellence of the Swiss watchmaking tradition and is often used by luxury brands.

33. https://www.richardmille.com/fr/page/rd (accessed on May 25, 2021).

34. *Vontobel Luxury Goods Shop*, Zurich: Vontobel, 2011; Edouard Aubin and Elena Mariani, *Swiss Watches*.

35. Tom Nicholas, *VC: an American history*, Cambridge: Harvard University Press, 2019.

BIBLIOGRAPHY

Annual reports of companies and associations

Audi, Brunello Cucinelli, Burberry, Chow Tai Fook, Christian Dior Couture, Compagnie financière Richemont, Contrôle officiel suisse des chronomètres, Hermès, Inditex, Kering, Kosé, L'Oréal, Louis Vuitton, LVMH, Michael Kors Holdings, Pandora, Pola Orbis, PVH, Ralph Lauren, Shiseido, Swatch Group, Titan Industries.

Newspapers and magazines

Europa Star, Feuille officielle suisse du commerce, Financial Times, Jewellery News Asia, Journal de Genève, Le Figaro, Le Monde, Le Temps, Les Echos, New York Times, Nikkei, South China Morning Post, The Guardian, The New Daily, The Wall Street Journal, Time, Washington Post.

Books and articles

Agins, Teri, *The End of Fashion: how marketing changed the clothing business for ever*, New York: Morrow, 1999.

Allérès, Danielle, "Spécificités et stratégies marketing des différents univers du luxe," *Revue française du marketing*, vol. 132, 1991, pp. 71–96.

Armbruster-Sandoval, Ralph, "Globalization and cross-border labor organizing: the Guatemalan maquiladora industry and the Phillips Van Heusen workers' movement," *Latin American Perspectives*, vol. 26, no. 2, 1999, pp. 108–28.

Armitage, John and Joanne Roberts (eds.), *Critical Luxury Studies: defining a field*, Edinburgh: Edinburgh University Press, 2016.

Aubin Edouard and Elena Mariani, *Swiss Watches: polarisation accelerates further*, Morgan Stanley & Co., 2020.

Audi AG, *A History of Progress: chronicle of the Audi AG*, Cambridge: Bentley Publishers, 1998.

Bain & Co., *Eight Themes That Are Rewriting the Future of Luxury Goods*, 2019, www.bain.com

Bain & Co., *From Surging Recovery to Elegant Advance: The Evolving Future of Luxury*, 2021, p. 14.

Berger, Molly W., *Hotel Dreams: luxury, technology, and urban ambition in America, 1829–1929*, Baltimore: Johns Hopkins University Press, 2011.

Bergeron, Louis, *Les industries de luxe en France*, Paris: Odile Jacob, 1998.

Bonetti Francesca, "Italian luxury fashion brands in China: a retail perspective," *The International Review of Retail, Distribution and Consumer Research*, vol. 24, no. 4, 2014, pp. 453–477.

Bonin, Hubert, "Reassessment of the Business History of the French Luxury Sector. The Emergence of a New Business Model and a Renewed Corporate Image (from the 1970s," in Segret Luciano et al. (eds.), *European Business and Brand Building*, Bruxelles: PIE Peter Lang, 2012, pp. 113–35.

Bonvicini, Stéphanie, *Louis Vuitton: une saga française*, Paris: Fayard, 2004.

Bibliography

Bourdieu, Pierre, *La Distinction: Critique sociale du jugement*, Paris: Éditions de Minuit, 1979.

Bouwens, Bram, Pierre-Yves Donzé, and Takafumi Kurosawa (eds.), *Industries and Global Competition: a history of business beyond borders*, New York: Routledge, 2017.

Briot, Eugénie, *La Fabrique des parfums: Naissance d'une industrie de luxe*, Paris: Vendémiaire, 2015.

Briot, Eugénie, "1921: Parfumer le monde," in Boucheron Patrick (eds.), *Histoire mondiale de la France*, Paris: Seuil, 2018, pp. 800–5.

Bytheway, Simon James, *Investing Japan: foreign capital, monetary standards, and economic development, 1859–2011*, Cambridge: Harvard University Asia Center, 2014.

Campagnolo, Diego and Camuffo, "Globalization and low-technology industries: The case of Italian eyewear," in Paul L. Robertson and David Jacobsond (eds.), *Knowledge Transfer and Technology Diffusion*, Cheltenham: Edward Elgar, 2011, pp. 138–61.

Carnevali, Francesca, "Fashioning luxury for factory girls: American jewelry, 1860–1914," *Business History Review*, vol. 85, no. 2, 2011, pp. 295–317.

Castarède, Jean, *Histoire du luxe en France: des origines à nos jours*, Paris: Éditions Eyrolles, 2011.

Cedrola, Elena and Ksenia Silchenko, "Ermenegildo Zegna: When family values guide global expansion in the luxury industry," in Byoungho Jin and Elena Cedrola (eds.), *Fashion Brand Internationalization: opportunities and challenges*, New York: Palgrave Pivot, 2016, pp. 31–64.

Chandler, Alfred D., *Scale and Scope: the dynamics of industrial capitalism*, Boston: Harvard University Press, 1990.

Chatriot, Alain, "La construction récente des groupes de luxe français: mythes, discours et pratiques," *Entreprises et histoire*, no. 1, 2007, pp. 143–56.

Chattopadhyay, Utpal and Pragya Bhawsar, "Effects of Changing Business Environment on Organization Performance: The Case of HMT Watches Ltd," *South Asian Journal of Business and Management Cases*, vol. 6, no. 1, 2017, pp. 36–46.

Colli, Andrea, *Edizione: The Story of the Benetton Holding Company, 1986–Present*, London: Third Millennium Publishing, 2017.

Colli, Andrea, Elisabetta Merlo, "Family business and luxury business in Italy (1950–2000)," *Entreprises et histoire*, vol. 1, 2007, pp. 113–24.

Colli, Andrea, Alberto Rinaldi, and Michelangelo Vasta, "The only way to grow? Italian Business groups in historical perspective," *Business History*, vol. 58, no. 1, 2016, pp. 30–48.

Colli, Andrea and Michelangelo Vasta, "Large and entangled: Italian business groups in the long run," *Business History*, vol. 57, no. 1, 2015, pp. 64–96.

Comité, Colbert, *Le Comité Colbert en 2014*, Paris: Comité Colbert, 2014.

COMTRADE, https://comtrade.un.org/data/

Crettaz, Bernard, *La beauté du reste. Confessions d'un conservateur de musée sur la perfection et l'enfermement de la Suisse et des Alpes*, Carouge: Éditions Zoé, 1993.

Da Silva Lopes, Teresa, *Global Brands: the evolution of multinationals in alcoholic beverages*, Cambridge: Cambridge University Press, 2007.

Daix, Pierre, *François Pinault: essai biographique*, Paris: Éditions de Fallois, 1998.

Deloitte, *Global Power of Luxury Goods 2019*, Deloitte Touche Tohmatsu Ltd., 2019.

Dion, Delphine, "How to manage heritage brands: the case of sleeping beauties revival," in Pierre-Yves Donzé, Joanne Roberts, and Véronique Pouillard, *Oxford Handbook of Luxury Business*, Oxford & New York: Oxford University Press, 2022, pp. 273–286.

Donzé, Pierre-Yves, "Global competition and technological innovation: a new interpretation of the watch crisis, 1970s–1980s," in Thomas David, Jon Mathieu, Janick Marina Schaufelbuehl, and Tobias Straumann (eds.), *Crises-Causes, interprétations et conséquences*, Zurich: Chronos, 2012, pp. 275–89.

Donzé, Pierre-Yves, *Histoire du Swatch Group*, Neuchâtel: Alphil, 2012.

Donzé, Pierre-Yves, *A Business History of the Swatch Group: the rebirth of Swiss watchmaking and the globalization of the luxury industry*, Basingstoke: Palgrave Macmillan, 2014.

Donzé, Pierre-Yves, *L'invention du luxe: histoire de l'horlogerie à Genève de 1815 à nos jours*, Neuchâtel: Alphil, 2017.

Donzé, Pierre-Yves, "Fashion watches: the emergence of accessory makers as intermediaries in the fashion system," *International Journal of Fashion Studies*, vol. 4, no. 1, 2017, pp. 69–85.

Donzé, Pierre-Yves, "How to enter the Chinese luxury market? The example of Swatch Group," in Pierre-Yves Donzé and Rika Fujioka (eds.), *Global Luxury: organizational change and emerging markets since the 1970s*, Singapore: Palgrave Macmillan, 2018, pp. 177–94.

Donzé, Pierre-Yves, "National labels and the competitiveness of European industries: the example of the 'Swiss Made' law since 1950," *European Review of History: Revue européenne d'histoire*, vol. 26, no. 5, 2019, pp. 855–70.

Donzé, Pierre-Yves, *Des nations, des firmes et des montres: histoire globale de l'industrie horlogère de 1850 à nos jours*, Neuchâtel: Alphil, 2020.

Donzé, Pierre-Yves, "Industrial Leadership and the Long-Lasting Competitiveness of the Swiss Watch Industry," in Martin Guttmann (ed.), *Historians on Leadership and Strategy: case studies from antiquity to modernity*, Cham: Springer, 2020, pp. 171–91.

Donzé, Pierre-Yves, "The transformation of global luxury brands: the case of the Swiss watch company Longines, 1880–2010," *Business History*, vol. 62, no. 1, 2020, pp. 26–41.

Donzé, Pierre-Yves, "Luxury as an industry," in Pierre-Yves Donzé, Joanne Roberts, and Véronique Pouillard, *Oxford Handbook of Luxury Business*, Oxford & New York: Oxford University Press, 2022, pp. 59–77.

Donzé, Pierre-Yves and David Borel, "Technological innovation and brand management: the Japanese watch industry since the 1990s," *Journal of Asia-Pacific Business*, vol. 20, no. 2, 2019, pp. 1–20.

Donzé, Pierre-Yves and Rika Fujioka, "Luxury business," *Oxford Research Encyclopedia Business and Management*, 2017, https://doi.org/10.1093/acrefore/9780190224851.013.96

Donzé, Pierre-Yves and Rika Fujioka (eds.), *Global Luxury: organizational cange and emerging markets since the 1970s*, Singapore: Palgrave Macmillan, 2018.

Donzé, Pierre-Yves and Rika Fujioka, "The formation of a technology-based fashion system, 1945–1990: the sources of the lost competitiveness of Japanese apparel companies," *Enterprise & Society*, forthcoming.

Donzé, Pierre-Yves, Sotaro Katsumata, "High-end luxury wine consumption and income inequality," *International Journal of Wine Business Research*, 2022, vol. 34, no. 1, pp. 112–32.

Donzé, Pierre-Yves and Shigehiro Nishimura (eds.), *Organizing Global Technology Flows: Institutions, Actors, and Processes*, New York: Routledge, 2014.

Donzé, Pierre-Yves and Ben Wubs, "LVMH: storytelling and organizing creativity in luxury and fashion," in Regina Lee Blaszczyk and Véronique Pouillard (eds.), *European Fashion: the creation of a global industry*, Manchester: Manchester University Press, 2018, pp. 63–85.

Donzé, Pierre-Yves and Ben Wubs, "Storytelling and the making of a global luxury fashion brand: Christian Dior," *International Journal of Fashion Studies*, vol. 6, no. 1, 2019, pp. 83–102.

Dufresnes, J.-L., "La maison Dior et le monde, 1946–2006," in *Christian Dior et le monde*, Paris: Artlys, 2006, pp. 5–9.

Duggan, Ginger Gregg, "The greatest show on earth: a look at contemporary fashion shows and their relationship to performance art," *Fashion Theory*, vol. 5, no. 3, 2001, pp. 243–70.

Eien No Bi Wo Motomete—POLA Monogatari, Tokyo: Pola, 1980.

Euromonitor International, https://go.euromonitor.com/passport.html

Eurostaf, Dafsa, *LVMH*, 1987.

Eveno, Patrick, "La construction d'un groupe international, LVMH," in Jacques Marseille (ed.), *Le luxe en France, du siècle des Lumières à nos jours*, Paris: Association pour le développement de l'histoire économique, 1999, pp. 291–321.

Fujioka, Rika, *Hyakkaten no seisei katei*, Tokyo: Yuhikaku, 2006.

Bibliography

Fujioka, Rika, "Kodoseichoki ni okeru hyakkaten no kokyuka to tokusen burando no yakuwari," *Keizai ronso*, vol. 187, no. 3, 2013, pp. 95–110.

Fujioka, Rika, Zhen Li, and Yuta Kaneko, "The democratization of luxury and the expansion of the Japanese market, 1960–2010," in Pierre-Yves Donzé and Rika Fujioka (eds.), *Global Luxury: organizational change and emerging markets since the 1970s*, Singapore: Palgrave Macmillan, 2018, pp. 133–56.

Gino, Francesca and Gary Pisano, "Humanistic Capitalism at Brunello Cucinelli," Harvard Business School Case 920–007, 2019.

Gistri, Giacomo, "Consumers, counterfeiters, and luxury goods," in Pierre-Yves Donzé, Véronique Pouillard, and Joanne Roberts (eds.), *Oxford Handbook of Luxury Business*, Oxford University Press, 2022, pp. 524–44.

Giroud, Françoise et al., *Dior: Christian Dior, 1905–1957*, Paris: Éditions du Regard, 1987.

Grau, François-Marie, *La haute couture*, Paris: PUF, 2000.

Hakala, U., S. Lätti, and B. Sandberg, "Operationalising brand heritage and cultural heritage," *Journal of Product & Brand Management*, vol. 20, no. 6, 2011, pp. 447–56.

Hall, J. R., "The time of history and the history of times," *History and Theory*, vol. 19, no. 2, 1980, pp. 113–31.

Halwani, Lama, "The online experience of luxury consumers: insight into motives and reservations," *International Journal of Business and Management*, vol. 15, no. 11, 2020, pp. 157–70.

Hata, Kyojiro, *Louis Vuitton Japon: L'invention du luxe*, Paris: Assouline, 2004.

Higgins, David M., *Brands, Geographical Origin, and the Global Economy: a history from the nineteenth century to the present*, Cambridge: Cambridge University Press, 2018.

Hines, Tony and Margaret Bruce, *Fashion Marketing*, Burlington: Butterworth-Heinemann, 2007.

Hobsbawm Eric and T Ranger. (eds.), *The Invention of Tradition*, Cambridge: Cambridge University Press, 1983.

JETRO, *Suisu no kinzoku-sei tokei bando: shijo chousa*, Tokyo: JETRO, 1980.

Kapferer, Jean-Noël, *Kapferer on Luxury: how luxury brands can grow yet remain rare*, New York: Kogan Page Publishers, 2015.

Kapferer, Jean-Noël and Vincent Bastien, *The Luxury Strategy*, New York: Kogan Page, 2009.

Interbrand, Best Global Brands 2020, https://www.interbrand.com/best-brands/

International Directory of Company Histories, 150 volumes, Farmington Hills: St. James Press, 1988–2014.

Jeannerat, Hugues and Olivier Crevoisier, "Non-technological innovation and multi-local territorial knowledge dynamics in the Swiss watch industry," *International Journal of Innovation and Regional Development*, vol. 3, no. 1, 2011, pp. 26–44.

Jones, Geoffrey, *Beauty Imagined: a history of the global beauty iIndustry*, Oxford: Oxford University Press, 2010.

Jones, Geoffrey and Véronique Pouillard, "Christian Dior: a New Look for haute couture," *HBS Case* 809–159, 2009.

Kinoshita, Akihiro, "Burando gainen no kakucho: 1970nendai Itokin no jirei," *Keizai ronso*, vol. 171, no. 3, 2003, pp. 1–20.

Kinoshita, Akihiro, *Apapreru sangyo no maketingushi: burando kochiku to kouri kino no hosetsu*, Tokyo: Dobunkan, 2011.

Lévi-Strauss, Claude, *La pensée sauvage*, Paris: Plon, 1962.

Madhavi, S. and T. Rama Devi, "Problems of Indian jewellery industry," *International Journal of Management Research and Reviews*, vol. 5, no. 8, 2015, pp. 623–8.

Marrou, Henri-Irénée, *De la connaissance historique*, Paris: Seuil, 1954.

Marseille, Jacques, *Le luxe en France du siècle des lumières à nos jours*, Paris: Association pour le développement de l'histoire économique, 1999.

Marseille, Jacques, *L'Oréal, 1909–2009*, Paris: Perrin, 2009.

Mendes, V. and A. de la Haye, *Fashion Since 1900*, London: Thames & Hudson, 2010.

Merlo, Elisabetta, "Italian fashion business: achievements and challenges (1970s–2000s)," *Business History*, vol. 53, no. 3, 2011, pp. 344–62.

Merlo, Elisabetta, "Italian luxury goods industry on the move: SMEs and global value chains," in Pierre-Yves Donzé and Rika Fujioka (eds.), *Global Luxury: organizational change and emerging markets since the 1970s*, Singapore: Palgrave Macmillan, 2018, pp. 60–1.

Merlo, Elisabetta and Mario Perugini, "Making Italian fashion global: brand building and management at Gruppo Finanziario Tessile (1950s–1990s)," *Business History*, vol. 62, no. 1, 2020, pp. 42–69.

Merlo, Elisabetta and Francesca Polese, "Turning fashion into business: The emergence of Milan as an international fashion hub," *Business History Review*, vol. 80, no. 3, 2006, pp. 415–47.

Messarovitch, Yves, *Bernard Arnault: la passion créative*, Paris: Plon, 2004.

Moore, Christopher, "The strategic value of the mono-brand store for European luxury fashion brands," in Pierre-Yves Donzé, Joanne Roberts, and Véronique Pouillard, *Oxford Handbook of Luxury Business*, Oxford & New York: Oxford University Press, 2022, pp. 353–77.

Moore, Christopher M. and Grete Birtwistle, "The Burberry business model: creating an international luxury fashion brand," *International Journal of Retail & Distribution Management*, vol. 32, no. 8, 2004, pp. 412–22.

Moore, Christopher M. and Grete Birtwistle, "The nature of parenting advantage in luxury fashion retailing: the case of Gucci Group NV," *International Journal of Retail & Distribution Management,* vol. 33, no. 4, 2005, pp. 256–70.

Nadelhoffer, Hans, *Cartier*, San Francisco: Chronicle Books, 2007.

Nicholas, Tom, *VC: an American history*, Cambridge: Harvard University Press, 2019.

Nieuwenhuis, Paul and Peter Wells (eds.), *The Global Automotive Industry*, Singapore: John Wiley & Sons, 2015.

Nueno, Jose Luis and John A. Quelch, "The mass marketing of luxury," *Business Horizons*, vol. 41, no. 6, 1998, pp. 61–8.

Oakley, Peter, "Searching for pure gold: the impact of ethical gold sourcing certification programmes in the UK and Switzerland," *Environmental Science & Policy*, vol. 132, 2022, pp. 101–8.

Okawa, Tomoko, "Licensing practices at Maison Christian Dior," in Regina Lee Blaszczyk (ed.), *Producing Fashion: commerce, culture, and consumers*, Philadelphia: University of Pennsylvania Press, 2008, pp. 82–110.

Ostillio, Maria Carmela and Sarah Ghaddar, "Tod's: a global multi-brand company with a taste of tradition," in Byoungho Jin and Elena Cedrola (eds.), *Fashion Brand Internationalization: opportunities and challenges*, New York: Palgrave Pivot, 2016, pp. 101–23.

Ostillio, Maria Carmela and Sarah Ghaddar, "Salvatore Ferragamo: brand heritage as main vector of brand extension and internationalization," in Byoungho Jin and Elena Cedrola (eds.), *Fashion Brand Internationalization: opportunities and challenges*, New York: Palgrave Pivot, 2016, pp. 73–99.

Piketty, Thomas, *Le capital au xxie siècle*, Paris: Seuil, 2013.

Piketty, Thomas, *Capital et idéologie*, Paris: Seuil, 2019.

Potvin, John, *Giorgio Armani: Empire of the Senses*, London & New York: Routledge, 2013.

Pouillard, Véronique, "Managing fashion creativity. The history of the Chambre Syndicale de la Couture Parisienne during the interwar period," *Investigaciones de Historia Económica-Economic History Research*, vol. 12, no. 2, 2016, pp. 76–89.

Pouillard, Véronique, *Paris to New York: the transatlantic fashion industry in the twentieth century*, Cambridge: Harvard University Press, 2021.

Pries, Ludger, "Accelerating from a multinational to a transnational carmaker: the Volkswagen consortium in the 1990s," in Michel Freyssenet, Koichi Shimizu, and Giuseppe Volpato (eds.),

Globalization or Regionalization of the European Car Industry? Basingstoke: Palgrave Macmillan, 2003, pp. 51–72.

Pronitcheva, Karina, "Luxury brands and public museums: from anniversary exhibitions to co-branding," in Pierre-Yves Donzé and Rika Fujioka (eds.), *Global Luxury: organizational change and emerging markets since the 1970s*, Singapore: Palgrave Macmillan, 2018, pp. 219–37.

Quek, Mary, "Comparative historical analysis of four UK hotel companies, 1979–2004," *International Journal of Contemporary Hospitality Management*, vol. 23, no. 2, 2011, pp. 147–73.

Re, Piergiorgio et al., "The role of the founder's DNA throughout crisis: the revitalization of Moncler," in Fabrizio Mosca et al. (eds.), *Global Marketing Strategies for the Promotion of Luxury Goods*, Hershey: IGI Global, 2016, pp. 266–83.

Richon, Marco, *Omega Saga*, Bienne: Fondation Brandt, 1998.

Rosen, Ellen Israel, *Making Sweatshops: the globalization of the US apparel industry*, Berkeley: University of California Press, 2002.

Rosenbaum, Mark S. and Daniel S. Spears, "An exploration of spending behaviors among Japanese tourists," *Journal of Travel Research*, vol. 44, no. 4, 2006, pp. 467–73.

Sadun, Raffaella, Hanoch Feit, Vaibhav Gujral, and Gerard Zouein, "Transforming Tommy Hilfiger (A)," Harvard Business School Case 714–451, 2014.

Salmon, Christian, *Storytelling: La machine à fabriquer des histoires et à formater les esprits*, Paris: La Découverte, 2007.

Savelli, Elisabetta, "Role of brand management of the luxury fashion brand in the global economic crisis: a case study of Aeffe group," *Journal of Global Fashion Marketing*, vol. 2, no. 3, 2011, pp. 170–9.

Schumpeter, Joseph, *Capitalism, Socialism and Democracy*, New York: Harper & Brothers, 1942.

Simmel, Georg, "Fashion," *International Quarterly*, vol. 10, 1904, pp. 130–55.

Smit, Barbara, *Pitch Invasion: Adidas, Puma and the making of modern sport*, London: Penguin UK, 2007.

Sombart, Werner, *Krieg und Kapitalismus*, Leipzig: Duncker & Humblot, 1913.

Stankeviciute, Rasa and Jonas Hoffmann, "The impact of brand extension on the parent luxury fashion brand: the cases of Giorgio Armani, Calvin Klein and Jimmy Choo," *Journal of Global Fashion Marketing*, vol. 1, no. 2, 2010, pp. 119–28.

Steele, Valerie, *Paris Fashion: a cultural history*, London: Bloomsbury Publishing, 1998.

Theurillat, Thierry and Pierre-Yves Donzé, "Retail networks and real estate: the case of Swiss luxury watches in China and Southeast Asia," *The International Review of Retail, Distribution and Consumer Research*, vol. 27, no. 2, 2017, pp. 126–45.

Trueb, Lucien F., *The World of Watches: history, industry, technology*, New York: Ebner Publishing, 2005.

Umemura, Maki and Stephanie Slater, "Reaching for global in the Japanese cosmetics industry, 1951 to 2015: the case of Shiseido," *Business History*, vol. 59, no. 6, 2017, pp. 877–903, p. 878.

Urde, M., S.A. Greyser, and J.M. Balmer, "Corporate brands with a heritage," *Journal of Brand Management*, vol. 15, no. 1, 2007, pp. 4–19.

Veblen, Thorstein, *The Theory of the Leisure Class: an economic study of institutions*, New York: Macmillan, 1899.

Vontobel Luxury Goods Shop, Zurich: Vontobel, 2011.

Vontobel Luxury Goods Shop, Zurich: Vontobel, 2018.

Wang, Ying, Shaojing Sun, Yiping Song, "Chinese luxury consumers: motivation, attitude and behavior," *Journal of Promotion Management*, vol. 17, no. 3, 2011, pp. 345–59.

Wiedmann, Klaus-Peter, P. Hennigs, S. Schmidt, and T. Wuestefeld, "The importance of brand heritage as a key performance driver in marketing management," *Journal of Brand Management*, vol. 19, no. 3, 2011, pp. 182–94.

Yamada, Masahiro, "Parasite singles feed on family system," *Japan Quarterly*, vol. 48, no. 1, 2001, pp. 10–16.

Zanon, Johanna, "Reawakening the 'sleeping beauties' of haute couture: the case of Guy and Arnaud de Lummen," in Regina Lee Blaszczyk, and Véronique Pouillard (eds.), *European Fashion: the creation of a global industry*, Manchester: Manchester University Press, 2018, pp. 86–115.

INDEX

Index